Harlan Hoge Ballard

Three Kingdoms

A handbook of the Agassiz Association

Harlan Hoge Ballard

Three Kingdoms
A handbook of the Agassiz Association

ISBN/EAN: 9783337247874

Printed in Europe, USA, Canada, Australia, Japan

Cover: Foto ©Andreas Hilbeck / pixelio.de

More available books at **www.hansebooks.com**

With great regard
Yours very truly
L Agassiz

Nahant, August 25,
1862.

THREE KINGDOMS

A HAND-BOOK OF THE
AGASSIZ ASSOCIATION

BY

HARLAN H. BALLARD
PRESIDENT OF THE ASSOCIATION

BRING US THE AIRS OF HILLS AND FORESTS,
THE SWEET AROMA OF BIRCH AND PINE,
GIVE US A WAFT OF THE NORTH-WIND LADEN
WITH SWEETBRIAR ODORS, AND BREATH OF KINE!
—WHITTIER

Seventh Thousand

NEW YORK
THE WRITERS PUBLISHING COMPANY
1888

PRESS OF FLEMING, BREWSTER & ALLEY,
81-33 W. TWENTY-THIRD ST., NEW YORK.

DEDICATED TO THE MEMORY OF

Louis Agassiz

IN THE HOPE OF LEADING MANY TO FOLLOW

IN HIS FOOTSTEPS

AUTHOR'S PREFACE.

THIS book is the child of necessity, and was made to serve instead of a personal reply to the inquiries concerning the Agassiz Association, which came more rapidly than pen could answer them. For about two years a list of all such questions was carefully kept, and then the answers were written here as concisely and accurately as possible. As the Association has grown the questions have increased in number and scope, so that with each new edition comes the necessity for an enlargement and revision of the book. The author has been so greatly assisted in its preparation and revision that he is now little more than its grateful editor, who begs to return his thanks to those whose kindness has contributed so essentially to the value of the book. Professor Hyatt has honored our work to the verge of flattery in his whole-hearted introduction. To Professors W. W. Bailey, of Providence, R. I.; T. H. McBride, of Iowa City, Ia., and William B Werthner, of Dayton, O., our readers are indebted for the valuable suggestions in botanical work. Professor W. O. Crosby has revised the chapter on the study of minerals. The Manhattan Chapter of the Agassiz Association has given assistance with regard to taxidermy. The List of Books could not have been properly prepared but for the co-operation of Professors McBride, Crosby, Stokes and Clarke; Geo. Bird Grinnell, Ph.D.; S. P. Sharples, State Assayer; Hilborne T. Cresson, and, particularly, Mr. O. Bjerregaard, of the Astor Library, and Dr. W. H. Seaman, who have diligently revised the entire list.

Other assistance is acknowledged in the text, and if among so many helpers any have failed of mention, it is not for lack of appreciation, but because the book is now in press and cannot be consulted. Finally, the author wishes to express his gratitude to the publishers for their hearty interest and most kind and courteous consideration.

PITTSFIELD, Mass., Jan. 14, 1888.

INTRODUCTION.

BOSTON SOCIETY OF NATURAL HISTORY,
Boston, Mass., Jan. 2, 1888.

THE WRITERS PUBLISHING COMPANY:

DEAR SIRS,—Having done me the honor to request that I should send you an introduction to your new edition of the Hand-book of the Agassiz Association, I have written out a few thoughts which I hope will be considered suitable for that purpose. I have also taken the liberty of making an appeal, which you had not requested me to do, but which I think ought to be made, in order to secure the future of the Association and the continuance of the good work it has begun.

If science has any moral strength, it lies in making the fearless pursuit of truth an end in itself, without reference to the ordinary limitations of expediency. Nevertheless, this higher mode of life, when carried to excess, has certain more or less injurious reactions upon the mind. The scientific recluse shut up in his own thoughts, as in a cell, and magnifying the grandeur and importance of his own work at the expense of that of others not exclusively devoted to research, is more nearly a modern imitator of the monastic original than most persons are apt to suppose. Three classes of men have been required for the accomplishment of the greater triumphs of science : the investigators or discoverers of abstract and often apparently useless truths, teachers of all grades, and popularizers. The great man after whom your organization has been named, Louis Agassiz, was in his younger days pre-eminently an investigator, later in life he became, perhaps even more, a teacher, and also a popularizer of natural history. He possessed faculties of rare power in all three directions, and, therefore, succeeded in making a deep and lasting impression upon the history of science, as well as upon the minds of the people. Before his day scientific men were looked upon as busy triflers ; after that time they had gained a certain standing in the eyes of the public, and in the permanent respect of the better educated classes. I have often heard him say that science in America could not prosper without the good-will and respect of the people.

Darwin's service to science would have been much slighter in its immediate effect had it not been for the multitude of teachers who echoed his voice in every institution of learning, and the lecturers who repeated his theme with infinite variations from every rostrum and newspaper throughout the civilized world.

Fortunately for the future of science in this country, there is now a daily increasing popular constituency. This has been largely gained by the unselfish and unrewarded efforts of investigators, and also by a growing disposition on their part to help forward all organizations having the education of the public in view. Though needing as much as other men the comforts of life, and having as great desire for the enjoyment of its luxuries, and feeling quite as keenly the need of making every effort remunerative, they have nevertheless not hesitated to sacrifice their valuable time that others might be better educated and the cause of scientific culture advanced.

Sooner or later in the history of institutions there comes a period of ripe development and increasing usefulness, which must be supported not only by those benefited—the members and patrons—but by larger income derived from invested funds or from the government. The work of the Agassiz Association is of vast importance to science, but if it were not dependent upon voluntary labor, its efficiency would be even greater than it is. It has already reached a period when provision should begin to be made for placing its work upon the more permanent basis of funded property and paid labor. That it is worthy of the support already received from its thousands of members cannot be questioned, and this is a sufficient guarantee that it would be a proper and useful trustee and administrator of a part of the large sums annually distributed by public-spirited persons to institutions having not a tithe of its claims to their favorable consideration.

The support now obtainable from legislators for the uses of science is hard to get, simply because they have, as individuals, no practical experience of the benefits of science-teaching, either in their own lives or those of their children. They allow themselves to be persuaded frequently into giving appropriations for the benefit of science, but they know that their constituents have little sympathy, and are even less disposed than themselves to allow the public money to be used for what seems to them purely æsthetical purposes. The arrival of the public at a stage of enlightenment and proper appreciation which must render the task of science lighter and more effective, will probably be much facilitated by the work of the Agassiz Association. The numerous chapters scattered throughout the land cannot fail to effect more or less of a revolution in the modes of life and thought of thousands of families, and through them sensibly affect many communities. Leaving out of sight all other effects, this influence alone would entitle the

Association to the support of scientific men. The labors of the Association are, however, entitled to serious consideration in other ways, and the actual results of the work done are as astonishing as the unprecedented quickness of growth of the Association in numbers and influence.

The originator of this enterprise has done something permanent toward developing and spreading a taste for self-culture in an almost new sense, so far as the majority of people are concerned. He has shown that there is a practicable method by which the average intelligence and self-reliant character of the people outside of the schoolroom, as well as in it, can be effectively increased. He has taught thousands how to work with whatever means were at hand, not only for their own intellectual improvement, but for that of their children and neighbors. This must also eventually affect the curriculum of the public schools in many places, through the creation of a demand for better and more natural methods of instruction. If he devote the remainder of his life to carrying on and perfecting the system he has originated, he can do nothing more desirable for the interests of science in this country, or more likely to secure future happiness and personal satisfaction for himself, as well as for many thousands of his country-people of all ages and both sexes.

I shall also take the liberty of saying that material returns should not be wanting, in order to secure the enjoyment of something more than the personal satisfaction of having done good work, and that the Association should be placed on a permanent basis, and its work secured, now and in the future, by means of large invested funds.

Respectfully yours,
ALPHEUS HYATT.

CONTENTS.

THREE KINGDOMS.

CHAPTER I.

THE Agassiz Association, for the observation and study of natural objects, was founded in 1875 by the writer, in connection with a school which he was then teaching in Lenox, Mass. It was the outgrowth of a life-long love for nature, and a belief that education is incomplete unless it include some practical knowledge of the common objects that surround us. For several years the little school society continued its work pleasantly and with profit. The president gradually came to the opinion (strengthened by reading an account of a somewhat similar, though far more limited, organization in Switzerland), that there might be other communities in which a like society would be welcomed, and several branch societies were organized. To test the matter more fully, having obtained the cordial co-operation of the editors of the *St. Nicholas*, a general invitation to unite in the work was published in 1880, in the November number of that magazine. It was substantially as follows:

THE INVITATION.

You must know that, across the ocean and over the Alps, the boys and girls of Switzerland have a bright idea. They have formed a society, and they have a badge. The badge is a spray of evergreen, and the society is a Natural History Society.

Once a year, in the spring-time, when the sun has lifted the ice-curtain from the lakes, so that the fishes can look out, and the flowers can look in, the children from far and near come together for a meeting and a holiday. They are the boys and girls for a tramp! Their sturdy legs and long staves, their strong bodies and short dresses, their gay stockings and stout shoes prove that beyond a question.

The long golden hair of the girls, tightly braided and firmly knotted with gay ribbons, flashes brightly as they go clambering over rocks, leaping across rivulets, scrambling along glaciers, and climbing steep cliffs.

When the village schoolmaster, who usually leads these excursions, blows his horn, back come the children, like laughing echoes, with baskets, pockets, boxes, and bags full of the treasures of the wood.

Then they eat their dinner as we would take a picnic, and after that, spread out their trophies, and decide who has found the most, and who the rarest. They get the master to name them, if he can, and laugh in mischievous triumph when he fails.

With the lengthening shadows, the children return to their homes, and arrange their mosses, ferns and flowers, their pebbles and beetles and butterflies, in cabinets, and declare, in their quaint accents, that they have had a glorious time. And have they not? The fresh, crisp air, the holiday, the sunshine, the picnic, the gathered specimens, and a teacher to tell them Latin names! No wonder they enjoy it. Would not you?

But, on reflection, we have all those things in this country, could we once bring them together in the right proportions. We have holidays enough—there are Saturdays. Schoolmasters are as plentiful as schools. This is the same sun that shines on Switzerland, and it can find golden hair to kindle, without waiting for the sea to turn under it. Why, then, cannot we have a Natural History Society in America? In fact, we already have a little one, up here in these Berkshire Hills. And we enjoy it so thoroughly, and learn so much from it, that we wish it to grow larger.

Not many of you need be told why we have named our Society THE AGASSIZ ASSOCIATION. There are few that have not heard something of the life and work of that famous man—so universally honored and beloved—Professor Louis Agassiz. In 1846 the great Naturalist left his native Switzerland, made America his home, accepted a Professorship at Harvard College, and built up the greatest school of Natural History in this country. Though one of the most learned, he was also one of the most devout and gentle of men.

Mrs. Agassiz, the widow of Louis Agassiz, and Professor Alexander Agassiz, his son, lend their cordial approval to our Society and its work, and have very kindly given us permission to use the father's name.

THE RESPONSE.

This invitation met a response at once gratifying and unexpected. A very general interest in the study of nature has been evinced by young and old. Classes or Chapters have been formed in different towns, under the direction of the central organization, and, where this has been impracticable, individuals have joined as corresponding members. Within seven years, more than fifteen thousand students have been aided, and more than twelve hundred local scientific societies established. Though originally planned as an aid to young people, the interest of the older ones has proved even greater, and we are gratified to find on our roll of membership the names of many fathers and mothers, teachers and professors. Several of our chapters are composed wholly of adults; many of old and young working together. Family Chapters are among our most successful branches.

SCHOOL SOCIETIES.

As the A. A. has become better known, it has found a wide field of usefulness in connection with schools, both private and public. Many teachers who have not been able to find a place for natural science in the ordinary curriculum, and who have yet felt that their pupils should not grow up strangers to the flowers, trees, birds and butterflies, have been glad to devote an hour once a fortnight to the guidance of a meeting devoted to these studies. In almost every school may be found, at the least, six of the more intelligent boys and girls who will willingly spend an evening now and then in united study and discussion. The young are naturally fond of collecting. Most school committees will cheerfully grant the use of a room for the meetings, and many will even provide suitable cases for the specimens. In each of the several hundred schools in which branches of the Agassiz Association have been organized, the resultant work of personal observation has had a marked tendency to counteract the evils of rote-work and routine. In most cases cabinets have been secured and have been filled with specimens collected by the pupils themselves within a radius of five miles of the school-house door. Visit such a society as the Agassiz Chapter in Greenfield, or Fitchburg, Mass.; or that in Davenport, Iowa; or that in Tacoma, Washington Territory; or that in Kioto, Japan, and ask to be shown representations of the local fauna, flora, or mineralia. The young men and women will show you collections carefully prepared, accurately labeled, diligently studied, highly valued, and exceedingly valuable. The Agassiz Association does not so much care for rarities or monstrosities. Our cabinets are neither junk-shops nor dime-museums. Our purpose is rather to learn about the stones by the roadside and in the quarry ; to become familiar with the plants we pass on our way to school, and with the insects that feed upon and fertilize them ; to get on speaking terms with, and out of all cruel relations to, each warbler of the orchard and the wildwood ; to discover what fishes swim in our brooks, what shells sing on our beaches and hide in our groves, what invisible animalcules live in our ponds and ditches, what stars shine in our sky. It was a dream of Louis Agassiz himself to see American youth early led into the pleasant paths of natural science ; to see them forsaking all foolish and wanton sport for the sake of a wise and loving study of the works of God.

Every teacher has at some time felt how delightful it would be if she could only lead her pupils to see the inexpressible beauty that lies hid from unawakened eyes in pebble, and leaf, and wing. But many have been discouraged from making any serious endeavor from fear of failure. It is better to try and fail, than fail for fear of trying. It must be admitted, however, that there are usually serious hindrances in the way. First of all many teachers feel that they are already working at too high a tension. Then, others, not having enjoyed special training in natural science, feel a modest reluctance about attempting to train others. In other cases it is found difficult to inspire and maintain among the young a strong and growing interest in these matters. The first of these objections can be met by making the association-work an avocation instead of a vocation ; a calling *from* work, instead of a calling *to* it. Take your pupils with you for an occasional afternoon, if you can get leave of absence ; and, my word for it, you and they will fare none the worse at the end of the term for the exchange of one or two grammar recitations, or examinations in geography, for a little practical knowledge of what lives and moves and has its being out of doors, and a few lung-fuls of crisp June or October oxygen.

Your own ignorance, if that is what you do own on these matters, will the better enable you to study with your pupils ; and next to instruction from the most gifted master, nothing is more inspiring than such friendly companionship in learning. As for failing to interest your pupils, remember that a taste for the pure pleasures of natural science, like a taste for olives, must be cultivated by persistent tasting! After one or two excursions, followed by a careful study of the specimens obtained, with the personal use of micro-scope or blowpipe, enthusiasm generally grows like purslane. You will find, too, that the Association will be a great help to you. We have now about fifty scientific specialists always ready to aid the members by answering their letters of inquiry, and by determin-ing their specimens for them, free of cost, save postage.

A boy in a grammar school in the uttermost parts of Dakota becomes interested in fishes. He finds the common varieties that he knows, and studies them. By and by he takes in his net or on his hook a stranger. He finds no account of him in the small zoölogy in the school library. The teacher cannot help him. He studies the fish with his eyes, examines fins, and scales, and skeleton. Then he prepares a description, as accurately as he can, perhaps aided in this by the teacher, and sends it with a rude sketch, it may be, to Dr. Holder, of the New York Central Park, who is one of the gentlemen who kindly assist our students. In a few days he receives a letter, giving him the name of his fish, and, what is better, the name of a book from which he can learn much more about fishes than from any volume that ever before found its way into his village. How he is encouraged by this graceful sympathy! He hoards his earnings till the book is bought. He studies it by candlelight after the chores are done. He masters it, and presents it to his little society, where it becomes the nucleus of a scientific library, which ten years from now may require a building to protect it. By the time this boy has finished school he knows more about the fish in the local waters than his parents or instructors, and he has become fired with ambition to go to some place where he can meet men who know enough to teach him more. He enters a college or higher scientific school, and becomes, before many years are gone, himself a specialist, ready, nay eager, to help other poor boys in other isolated places. This is no fancy sketch, but has been realized over and over again since the Agassiz Association was founded in 1875.

SPECIAL CLASSES.

Among the pleasant features of the A. A. have been our special courses of study. These have been conducted by men high in their departments, and have always been free. Dr. Marcus E. Jones, of Salt Lake City, has taken a class through elementary botany; Prof. G. Howard Parker has directed a six-months' course in entomology; Prof. E. L. French, of Wells College, has managed a very successful course of botanical collecting and exchange; and Prof. W. O. Crosby, of the Boston Society of Natural History, has conducted two classes, each of one hundred and fifty pupils, through highly interesting courses in the elements of determinative mineralogy. All these gentlemen have most generously volunteered their services, and we cannot but hope that others will be found to imitate their example of true philanthropy. One of the most urgent needs of the Association is the volunteer assistance of competent men to conduct in botany, biology, entomology, and chemistry courses of study on a plan similar to that so successfully inaugurated by the gentlemen just now named.

THE PLAN OF THE ASSOCIATION.

From this brief sketch of the origin and work of the A. A., the purpose of its founder may be fairly inferred. The Association was designed to be an extended free school of natural science open to persons of all ages and conditions. Local classes, or chapters, were to be formed, quite independent of each other, and of the President, except in so far as by adopting a common name, and by a facility of inter-correspondence and exchange, they might render to each other mutual encouragement and aid; and by correspondence with the President, receive such guidance as he should be able to give them.

As it has been our constant intention to have the A. A. relieved from all machinery, politics, and red tape, we have adopted the following extremely simple Constitution, which gives us just enough cohesion to stimulate an *esprit de corps*, but leaves each class, or chapter, absolutely free from any jurisdiction whatever.

CONSTITUTION.

Art. 1. The name of this Society shall be *The Agassiz Association.*

Art. 2. It shall be the object of this Association to collect, study, and preserve natural objects and facts.

Art. 3. The officer of this Association shall be a President, who shall perform the customary duties of such officer, and who may nominate his own successor, who may be elected by the votes of a majority of the chapters of the Association.

Art. 4. New chapters may be added with the consent of the President, provided that no such chapter shall consist of less than four members. Chapters shall be named from the towns in which they exist, and, if there be more than one chapter in a town, they shall be further distinguished by the letters of the alphabet.

Art. 5. Each chapter may choose it own officers, and make its own by-laws.

Art. 6. *The Swiss Cross* shall be the official organ of the Agassiz Association.

Art. 7. This Constitution may be amended by a three-fourths vote of the Association or its representatives.

The wisdom of this plan of organization seems to be established by the rapid growth and increasing prosperity of the Association.

ADVANTAGES.

The advantages which may result from the formation of a branch in the family or school far outweigh the labor and time required. Habits of observation are formed ; valuable knowledge is acquired ; spontaneous study is secured ; health-giving rambles are taken ; the elements of parliamentary law are learned and practiced ; subjects for compositions are abundantly supplied ; power of debate is attained ; practice in letter-writing is necessitated ; valuable collections are made ; useful libraries are founded ; pleasant acquaintances are formed ; windows are opened into distant States, through which we catch glimpses of scenery new to us ; we see various strange forms of animal and plant life ; we read fossil records of the past ; we become acquainted with the modes of thought and expression which prevail outside our own homes. Correspondence with chapters in different States is like the magical glass of the Arabian prince.

Sitting by our study-table, we can see in every direction sturdy boys and graceful girls, searching

eagerly for nature's hidden treasures. We see them
scouring the prairies of Kansas; climbing the foot-
hills of the Sierras; discovering beautiful caves in the
Rocky Mountains; analyzing magnolia blossoms in
Mississippi; killing rattlesnakes on their own door-
steps in Colorado; studying geology in England;
gathering edelweiss from the slopes of the Alps;
wandering, by permit, through New York's Central
Park; spying out specimens from the mica mines of
Vermont; picking up tarantulas and scorpions in
Texas; searching for the flowers and insects of the
Argentine Republic; gathering algæ and sea-shells on
the coast of Florida; growing wise in the paleontology
of Iowa; arranging the variously colored sands of the
Mississippi river in curious bottles; in Massachusetts,
anxious to know whether "the *Limnanthemum* of our
waters has roots;" sending from Chicago to learn
about the centre of buoyancy; holding field-meetings
in Illinois; celebrating the birthday of Professor
Agassiz (May 28), in many States, with a picnic and
appropriate exercises; giving entertainments and real-
izing enough to buy a cabinet and have thirty dollars
over to start a library in Oregon; making wonderful
collections in Virginia; enjoying the assistance and
listening to the lectures of eminent scientists in Philadelphia; enrolling scholars and teachers in Connecti-
cut and Rhode Island; determining to become professors in the District of Columbia; writing fraternal
messages from Canada; selecting quartz crystals from
the hot springs of Arkansas; discovering *Geastrums*
on Long Island; and everywhere learning to detect
the beautiful in the common, and the wonderful in
the before despised.

CHAPTER II.

WE will now proceed to answer the most important and constant questions that come to us from day to day. Naturally the first inquiry is, " How can I form a chapter of the A. A.?"

As four is the smallest number of persons recognized as a chapter, the first thing to do is to find at least three persons besides yourself who are interested in the plan. Call a meeting and appoint a temporary chairman. Explain to your friends the purpose for which you have called them together, and make a motion to the effect that a chapter of the A. A. be organized. If this motion prevails, it will be well to have a committee appointed to draft your by-laws, or the rules by which your chapter is to be guided. After choosing this committee you may adjourn.

At the next meeting, hear and act upon the report of your committee, and elect your permanent officers. It will prove of great service to you to conduct your meetings, as far as may be, in accordance with parliamentary law. Your by-laws should contain an article stating what authority shall control you in this regard. You will find ' Roberts' Rules of Order ' an excellent and intelligent guide. If you have no book of rules, the following will be found to cover the principal points which may perplex you :

RULES OF ORDER.

1. A quorum of members is always required for the transaction of business, and in the absence of a

special law, a majority of the members constitutes a quorum.

2. There is properly no business before the house until a member has been recognized by the chairman as having offered a motion.

3. It requires a two-thirds vote to suppress a question without permitting debate.

4. A motion to reconsider a question once decided can only be made by one who has voted affirmatively.

5. A rule adopted must be enforced by the chair without question.

6. Motions to lay on the table, and for the previous question, are customary methods for disposing of questions and abridging debate.

7. Debate must be confined to the question, and personalities are out of order.

8. Motions which are undebatable are : The previous question ; to lay on or take from the table ; an objection to the consideration of any question ; an appeal relative to indecorum or violation of rule ; questions relative to the order of business, to the withdrawal of a motion, to reading papers, or to suspending the rules ; and motions to adjourn, to fix the time to which to adjourn, or to postpone indefinitely. None of these can be amended except that to fix the time to which to adjourn. Precedence is given to motions in the following order ; and any motion, except to amend, can be made while one of a lower order is pending, but none can supersede one of a higher order :

1. To fix the time to which to adjourn.
2. To adjourn.
3. A call for the order of the day.
4. To lay on the table.
5. The previous question.
6. To postpone to a certain time.
7. To commit, amend, or postpone indefinitely.

BY-LAWS.

Very much of the comfort and harmony of your meetings will depend upon the wisdom of your by-laws. They should be simple, short, and comprehensive, and should cover such points as what officers you will have, how long they shall hold office, what initiation fee you will require, how many members you will admit, what fines, if any, you will impose for absence, what duties shall devolve upon your officers and members, and what order of exercises you will follow in your meetings. The following schedule may prove serviceable as a suggestion :

1. The name of this society shall be —.
2. The officers shall be —.
3. The entrance fee shall be —.
4. The regular dues shall be —.
5. The order of exercises at all regular meetings shall be : *a.* Roll-call ; *b.* Minutes of last meeting ; *c.* Treasurer's report ; *d.* Report of corresponding secretary ; *e.* Reports of members, on specimens, etc. ; *f.* Miscellaneous business ; *g.* Adjournment.
6. New members may be elected at any regular meeting of the society, by ballot, and — adverse votes shall exclude.
7. The meetings of this society shall be conducted in accordance with the rules of order contained in —.

Each chapter is expected to have a by-law to the effect that its secretary shall send to the President of the A. A. a carefully prepared *annual report* on the date assigned by its charter, and that, should the chapter at any time disband, immediate notice shall be sent to the President. Full directions for these annual reports are given on another page.

Some chapters have a by-law requiring each member to support our official organ, *The Swiss Cross*, but all these matters are left to local option. It is well, in a final section, to define the manner in which your by-laws may be amended.

The second article, concerning officers, should contain a clause limiting the time during which the various offices may be held ; but as the address of your president or secretary is to be published in *The Swiss Cross* and in the *Official Register*, for the benefit of other chapters, those officers should be made permanent if possible. In any case, you should decide on some address for the chapter, which may remain unaltered, whatever official changes may occur. *This matter of an exact and permanent address is of the highest importance.*

In societies where members are of nearly the same age, the decision of the majority should be regarded as absolute, and be cheerfully agreed to by the minority. In family chapters, and those under the direction of a teacher, it is well to have a by-law giving the president the power of veto, and making a three-fourths vote necessary to pass a motion over his veto. Such branches may, if they choose, constitute simple classes, and remain entirely subject to the control of parent or teacher. The Constitution leaves each branch entirely free in these matters.

The first duty of your secretary, after having recorded the minutes of your meeting for organization, will be to send to the President of the Association an account of the formation of the chapter, giving the date of organization, the names and addresses of your officers, and the names and ages of all your members. Once a year thereafter, a report of progress will be expected, and we shall also be glad to hear from every chapter informally at any time. The nature of this annual report can best be learned by a study of those presented hereafter in this book, but a few words of explanation here may be acceptable.

ANNUAL REPORTS.

In order to give each chapter fair opportunity to acquaint the Association with its progress, methods, and plans, the Association has been divided into *centuries*, consisting of one hundred chapters each. The chapters of the first century, numbers 1 to 100 inclusive, are to report on the 1st of January annually ; those of the second century, on the 1st of February, etc. The time when the report of any chapter falls due may be seen from the following table, only premising that the reports should be in the President's hands by or before the dates given :

1st Century, Chapters	1–100.	Annual report due		Jan. 1
2d " "	101–200.	"	"	Feb. 1
3d " "	201–300.	"	"	March 1
4th " "	301–400.	"	"	April 1
5th " "	401–500.	"	"	May 1
6th " "	501–600.	"	"	June 1
7th " "	601–700.	"	"	July 1
8th " "	701–800.	"	"	Oct. 1
9th " "	801–900.	"	"	Nov. 1
10th " "	901–1,000.	"	"	Dec. 1

If reports reach us promptly on the dates specified, we shall be enabled to print them, in whole or part, in the succeeding issue of *The Swiss Cross.* It will be observed that we call for the reports of the *eighth* century, Chapters 701–800, on or before October 1, instead of August 1. The reason for this is that we wish to allow two months for the summer vacation, which is now almost universally enjoyed by our schools and colleges. Besides this general notification, we shall indicate each month in *The Swiss Cross* the chapters which are to report the month following, and we shall also, for a time, send notices to the secretaries by mail. Having thus done our part by way of reminders, we shall rely on the chapters to see to it that their annual reports are properly prepared and promptly forwarded. We have been asked with regard to reports from chapters, whether they are limited to annual reports. Not at all. We are glad to hear from every chapter and from every member just as often as they feel moved to write. The number of chapters is so great that we cannot undertake to publish a report from each in *The Swiss Cross* oftener than once a year, but additional reports, notes, or letters may be sent at any time, and will always receive prompt attention. Every communication received is promptly answered ; so if you fail to receive a reply within a reasonable time, say ten days from time of mailing your letter if you live east of the Mississippi, you may safely conclude that the letter has been lost in the mails, and write again.

These annual reports should never be hastily prepared, nor deferred until the latest possible moment. Each chapter has, once a year, a fair chance to set forth its work and its results. A careless secretary may injure the standing of an excellent chapter. Most of the reports sent us are admirable, and show conscientious preparation.

In response to numerous inquiries as to the nature of the reports desired, we will say :

First, we wish *some* kind of report from *every* chapter. Even if you send only six words on a postal card, it will suffice to advise the Association of your existence and address. If you can say only, " Chapter 993 still lives ! " that is infinitely better than no report. Even if you should be obliged to report, " Chapter Blank is dead," the communication of the intelligence, unfortunate as it would be, would save the rest of us much uncertainty, confusion, labor, and expense.

Second, the annual report should contain a complete list of all changes in membership that may have occurred since your latest report.

Third, the annual report should give a brief summary of the year's work, number of meetings held, excursions made, entertainments given, special plans executed.

Fourth, the annual report should contain a brief account of the most interesting facts learned during the year by the personal observation of the chapter or any of its members. This is the point most frequently overlooked, yet it is second to none in importance. No society can work faithfully for a year without learning something which has interested its members, and which must, therefore, prove of interest to the Association at large. We recommend each chapter to bear constantly in mind, during the year, its next annual report. Let there be a large envelope labeled, "Items for next Annual Report," and into this let the secretary or any member, from time to time, drop slips of paper containing such facts as may be incorporated into the report. You will be astonished, at the end of the year, to discover what a wealth of material will have been accumulated. Let this, then, be carefully sifted and nicely arranged, and you will have an interesting and worthy report.

Fifth, when possible, let pictures accompany your reports. A sketch of some rare plant found last autumn, a photograph of your cabinet, or room ; in a word, a good picture of anything that has proved specially interesting and instructive to you. The use of the camera as an aid to science can hardly be overestimated, and it brings accurate picture-making within the capacity of nearly all.

INDIVIDUAL MEMBERS.

It frequently happens that an individual wishes to join the A. A., but is not able to interest enough companions to form a chapter. To provide for such persons, we allow them to become corresponding members of the Association on payment of a registration fee of 50 cents, and the purchase of this book. There are no subsequent dues.

Those who join us as corresponding members, are expected to work in their chosen departments, and to send to the President, once in two months, a concise report of their progress, modeled somewhat after the letters given later in the Hand-book. They enjoy all the privileges of charter members, except voting, and are at liberty to correspond and exchange with members of the regular chapters.

Four or more persons in different towns may unite by correspondence to form a chapter, and shall then be entitled to all the privileges of ordinary chapters.

CHAPTER III.

THE leaders of those chapters that desire to study the scientific classification of the objects of nature will do well to follow some such method as this : Consider, first, the three great kingdoms—Animal, Vegetable and Mineral. Let one meeting be devoted to the study of each as a kingdom. Let all the objects in your collection be classified so far as to determine regarding each, whether it belongs to the first, second, or third of these kingdoms. Determine the same regarding a multitude of substances—as air, water, milk, sugar, amber, alcohol, ink, paper, steel, paint, silk, flannel, steam, smoke, coal, kerosene, vinegar, etc.

Next take up the branches into which the several kingdoms are subdivided. These are for animals :

I. Protozoa.	V. Anthropoda.
II. Cœlenterata.	VI. Molluscoidea.
III. Echinodermata.	VII. Mollusca.
IV. Vermes.	VIII. Tunicata.

IX. Vertebrata.

Let these be carefully studied one by one, and thoroughly discussed, and illustrated by specimens, until any animal can readily be referred to its proper branch. If the books which contain this later classification are not at your command, you will do very well with the older divisions after Cuvier, viz.:

I. Vertebrates.	III. Mollusks.
II. Articulates.	IV. Radiates.

V. Protozoans.

These you will find in ordinary text-books. For chapter libraries, and for all who can afford it, I know of no better general work than the Standard Natural History, in six octavo volumes.

The divisions of the Vegetable kingdom are variously given by different authors. For the great majority of students the text-books by Wood and Gray will prove sufficient. Gray's Manual and Wood's Manual will be useful to more advanced students, while professional botanists must, of course, have recourse to various works in French, German, and Latin. Special works will be referred to in the chapter on 'Books Recommended.' The divisions and subdivisions of the Vegetable kingdom will become intelligible to the student as he progresses, and need no mention here.

The Mineral kingdom is divided into Metallic and Non-metallic substances, and these again comprise objects which exhibit different degrees of hardness, fusibility, specific gravity, etc., regard being had also to their chemical composition, and their peculiar forms of crystallization. Dana's Mineralogy is a good guide, and Brush's 'Determinative Mineralogy and Blowpipe Analysis' is an excellent manual for more advanced students, while beginners cannot do better than get Mrs. Ellen H. Richards' 'First Lessons on Minerals' and Professor Crosby's 'Tables for the Determination of Common Minerals.'

One object of this division and subdivision in the several kingdoms is so to classify all natural objects that we may determine the precise name of any specimen we may find. The more minute the subdivision, the more difficult often becomes the analysis. Thus, it is usually an easy matter to distinguish between an animal and a vegetable. It is not difficult to determine whether we are examining an insect or a worm.

If we find an insect, we may presently refer it to the *Lepidoptera*, and then to the butterflies : but when it comes to distinguishing between the various *Vanessas*, with their curious punctuation marks, the matter grows more serious, and we are compelled to obtain a book more restricted in scope than a zoölogy, and, indeed, than most entomologists.

As a result of this, it becomes necessary for him that would accurately study any department of nature to limit himself early to a small field.   One will choose, for instance, dragon-flies, and by devoting years to them will become a specialist and an authority in that department.   It is the tendency of the times to produce specialists.

Many persons, however, are not willing to restrict themselves to so narrow a field of study.   They prefer to range freely over mountain and along stream ; and having acquired the power to analyze a flower or determine a mineral, they leave the one to nod and smile on its dewy stem in undissected beauty, and the other to sparkle in the sunlight, instead of crackling in the reducing flame of a compound blowpipe.   Yet we must have strict scientists, and we honor the men who for the sake of expanding the world's knowledge are willing to confine their own researches to a narrow field.

For those, then, who are old enough to pursue a systematic course, we have briefly outlined a plan which may be followed in any department of natural science.   It consists in first obtaining a general view of the whole field, and then in learning its successive subdivisions, until analysis is complete.

The rest of you, and especially you, my little folk of ten years old and under, may, for the present, leave the big books unopened, and the Latin names unlearned.   Watch the minnows dart about in the crystal water; count the daisy flowers, and may they prove oracles of joy; blow off the dandelion's plumes to see if mother wants you; test your love for butter by the glimmer of the buttercup beneath your chins; find pretty pebbles by the brook, and keep them bright in glasses of water; gather brilliant autumn leaves, and press them for the days when their colors will be in the sky; study the beautiful crystals of the snow, lightly falling on your sleeve as you plod to school; learn to love the music of the rain, and the singing of the wind, and the moaning of the sea. You may not discover many wonderful things—or things that you will recognize as wonderful. But if the boys and girls in all the different places visited by *The Swiss Cross* were to tell each other about the common things in each one's own vicinity, there would be wonder enough, I am sure.

Yet you may find something altogether new. Did not little Maggie Edward find a new fish for her father? What? Never heard of Thomas Edward— the dear old shoemaker who use to make 'uppers' all day, and then lie all night in a hole in a sand-bank, with his head and gun out, watching for 'beasts?' In that case, you would do well to read the book called 'The Scotch Naturalist,' by Samuel Smiles.

Nature must be studied out-of-doors. Natural objects must be studied from the specimens themselves. The rocks must be broken open, the flowers must be studied as they grow, and animals must be watched as they live freely in their own strange homes. Quaint old Bernardin de St. Pierre, author of 'Paul and Virginia,' says :

"Botanists mislead us. They must have magnifying-glasses and scales in order to class the trees of a forest! To show me the character of a flower, it is presented to me dry, discolored, and spread out on

the leaf of an herbary. Who can discover the queen
of the flowers in a dried rose? In order to its being
an object at once of love and philosophy, it must be
viewed when, issuing from the cleft of a humid rock ; it
shines on its native verdure, when the zephyr sways
it, on a stem armed with thorns."

*Nothing can take the place of personal contact with
nature.* No great naturalist has learned his lessons
from books only.

Agassiz had learned more about fishes before he
ever saw a fish-book, than he found in the book after
he got it.

Audubon lived in the woods, and learned the voices
of all the birds, and could tell them also by their
flight.

Gilbert White wrote charming letters about the
swallows under his eaves, the cricket on his hearth
and the old tortoise that lived in his kitchen-garden.

W. W. Bailey braves the frosts of winter, and rambles
by the icy brooks, or through the snow-carpeted aisles
of the naked forest, to see what nature does when
summer is ended.   He writes :

"The pretty little stream is bordered by a fringe of
white ice, under which we can see great bubbles press,
squeezing themselves into very curious forms.   The
stream murmurs some pleasant story of the summer
violets.   On its still pools float leaf-gondolas of curious patterns.   Great fern-feathers, unwithered by the
frost, droop over the brook, and velvety mosses cushion
the shores."

These men understand Nature.   They enter into the
spirit of her mighty, throbbing life, and interpret the
secrets of her wondrous love.

And if you have ever known what it is to feel a
great love for the very earth, so that on some sunny
day you have wandered off alone, and under the

fragrant shade of an ancient pine, have thrown yourself upon her broad bosom, like a tired child ; or if,
when the wind was bending the long grass, you have
lain among the daisies, like Robert Falconer, watching your kite floating far up in the blue sky, and
wondering what there is beyond the kite, and beyond
the sky ; or if, on some dark day in December, when
gray clouds were skurrying across the sky, you have
climbed a hill alone, and from a swaying perch in a
leafless beech watched the drifting snow as it wrapped
the world in ermine—then you may believe that a
portion of the spirit that animated Agassiz, and
Edward, and Audubon, and White, and Wordsworth,
has fallen upon you.

CHAPTER IV.

HOW TO START A MUSEUM.

A MUSEUM may be a source of constant pleasure, or the cause of perpetual annoyance. All depends upon the purpose with which it is started, and the manner in which it is managed. Before giving advice as to the best way of making a museum permanently enjoyable, I will mention some of the most common causes of failure.

1. Many fail because they start their museum "just for fun." It is true that a great deal of pleasure can be got from a collection, but not when amusement is made the main purpose.

2. Others fail because they think that a museum is the same thing as a curiosity shop, and seek only those things that are quaint or rare. They want something that will make their friends open wide their eyes, and they like to have people ask, in surprise, " Why, where in the world did you get that ? "

3. A third cause of failure is the attempt to collect all sorts of things at once. You shall see, crowded together on the same shelf, coins, stamps, Indian relics, birds' eggs, autographs, sharks' teeth, sand from the Mississippi, wood from the home of Walter Scott, sea-beans, and pieces of the funeral decorations in memory of Lincoln or Garfield. In this way, the mind, confused and wearied, soon loses its interest.

4. An equally fatal error is the neglect to learn all that can be learned about each specimen. This usually follows the first and second sources of failure already mentioned. It sometimes results from a selfish spirit of gain, an inordinate love of possession.

I once had a boyish craze for coin-collecting. My chief motive was to see how many I could get ; to get more and rarer ones than my friend Jack had. When Jack and I parted to go to different schools, our rivalry ceased, and with it, my numismatic zeal withered away.

In later years, while looking at the remains of my collection, I became interested in a coin of Trajan. On one side was the head of the Emperor ; on the reverse, the Temple of Janus, and this inscription in Latin : "The Roman people, having secured peace on land and sea, has closed Janus." Coming, then, to look at coins as a means of verifying and vivifying history, my old enthusiasm instantly revived, and having now a reasonable rooting, became permanent.

5. Many young persons suppose that it is of paramount importance to know the name of every specimen. Therefore, finding it difficult to ascertain all names at once, they become discouraged and give up their purpose.

6. Finally, a mercenary few collect, hoping to sell again. It is needless to say that they are usually disappointed in this hope, and that whether or not they succeed in making money, they utterly fail of reaping the true benefits we propose for them from their home museum.

This mention of some of the more common causes of failure anticipates by contrast the sources of success. A museum should be started for the purpose of learning by personal observation, or of furnishing an opportunity for others to do so. Resolutely excluding the curiosity-shop idea, the collector should first definitely decide what kind of a museum he will make.

To aid him in this, I will indicate several distinct sorts of museums, adapted to persons of different tastes.

1. An unlimited collection ; usually unfortunate.

2. A collection *limited as to place.* For example, all the different specimens that can be found in a given county, in a certain township, by the banks of some stream, or on a selected mountain.

3. A collection *limited as to time.* As coins between 1776 and 1861 ; or specimens found between May and September.

4. A collection limited in kind, *e. g.*, minerals, stamps, ferns, beetles, seeds, snow-crystals.

5. Collections limited in two or more of these ways ; as, for example, flowers that blossom on Mt. Washington in June ; the varieties of quartz that occur in your own town ; the insects that visit your rosebush during one year.

6. Group-collections, by which I mean collections of objects of the same general kind ; and in connection therewith, other objects naturally grouped with them. To illustrate, suppose a tree-collection. If you begin with the chestnut, you might get a piece of the wood, showing the grain ; then you would group about this specimens of the chestnut bark, leaves, flowers, and fruit. You would add all the varieties of moss that grow on the tree, all insects that frequent and injure it, perhaps a sketch of the entire tree, and whatever else you might conceive to be naturally connected with it.

One variety of group-collection might be called a Development-collection, by which I mean a collection that shows different stages of growth. If you wished to show the progress in methods of lighting, you could arrange a series containing a pine-knot, a rush-light, tallow dip, wax taper, whale-oil lamp, fluid lamp, kerosene lamp, gas-fixtures, and the arc and incandescent electric lights. Or to illustrate the life-history of an insect, you could have a series of specimens beginning

with the egg, and continued through the various forms
of the caterpillar after his moultings, the cocoon and
chrysalis, to the perfect *imago*.

So, with a plant, an interesting group would represent its growth from seed to plumule, and through the
succeeding daily forms to bud and flower and fruit,
and back again to seed.

Another variety of group-collection shows the several stages in the manufacture of common substances.
Beginning with the cotton-boll, you would have the
ginned cotton, the thread, and various kinds of fabrics
that are woven from it ; starting again with the stalk
and flower of flax, you would have the soft, inner,
fibrous bark, the linen thread, linen and paper made
therefrom, also the seeds, and linseed-oil pressed out
of them, the linseed meal obtained by grinding the
oil-cake left after the oil has been expressed, and the
various other valuable products that make flax so
necessary to our comfort.

7. The last sort of museum that I will mention may
be called the Type-collection. This is a collection of
typical specimens chosen to illustrate the branches,
classes, genera, and other divisions into which objects
are classified. Following the popular system, there
might be in the Animal kingdom, a cat to represent
the vertebrates ; a lobster for the Articulates ; an
oyster for the Mollusks ; for the Radiates, a star-fish ;
and for the Protozoans, a sponge. Of course the
classification may be carried to any extent you choose ;
but you would need only a few type-specimens in each
division.

These must be considered merely as illustrations of
the different kinds of museums that may be made.
They range from the unlimited ' *Omnium gatherum*,'
which, I fear is the most common, as well as the most
unsatisfactory, through all the degrees of limitation.

Having decided what kind of museum you will have, the question arises, how to get your specimens.

The best, because the most profitable and enjoyable method, is by personal search. This is particularly true of the fifth and sixth classes of museums. The same sort of pleasure attends this plan that attends the sports of fishing and hunting ; and the same qualities—keenness, caution, and patience—are developed. The next best plan is by a system of exchanges.

The worst plan (except stealing) is to buy your specimens. Here, however, an exception must be made if you are making a collection of manufactured articles, or are arranging for a regular course of study.

Having secured your specimens, they must be prepared for the cabinet. Many excellent manuals are published containing full instructions for this preparation. If you can get the advice and example of some competent person, it will be still better.

For the reception of your treasures, the variety of cases is great. Let security and simplicity be chiefly sought. Boys who are not contented without showy and elaborate cases, seldom make valuable collections. It is not the boy with the fifty-dollar rod that catches the largest trout.

In arranging specimens, give each the largest practicable space. Do not huddle them. Nearly all kinds of specimens look well set on separate blocks of wood, neatly covered with white paper. Each one thus placed has an individuality obtainable by no other plan. Insects, eggs, mosses, shells, fossils, and minerals all appear to great advantage in this way. To retain the eggs in position, set each one on a little ball of putty, and press it gently until it forms a little socket for itself. Most oölogists, however, keep eggs in sets in the proper nests.

Cultivate neat habits. Leave no *débris* for mother

to take care of. Allow no disagreeable odors in the room. Keep all glass brightly polished. Keep every tool in its proper place. Remove all traces of dust. A distinguished scientist tells me that he makes many tests and analyses in his parlor, and that by attending to the matter, he does not make enough dirt to soil his handkerchief.

Do not make your museum a nuisance. Many great naturalists have erred here. Enthusiasm for science is not a valid excuse for forgetting the feelings of others. Remember that although you have no foolish fear of snakes, it may be very cruel in you to expect your sister to share your unconcern; and that although you may have grown indifferent to the fumes of stale and slimy alcohol, it may cause your mother serious distress.

Finally, do not keep your museum simply as an ornament. Study your specimens, and give others a chance to study them. Put up for a notice "Hands on," rather than "Hands off." Classify your collection as well as you can, but remember that classification is not the most important thing. Take your specimens one by one, and look at them, taste them, smell them, feel of them, and learn their properties by personal observation.

HOW TO MAKE A CABINET.

In 'Rollo's Museum,' a charming little book by Jacob Abbot, we read that Jonas made an excellent cabinet for Rollo, from a large packing-box. He stood it on end, fitted it with shelves, and closed it by doors attached by means of leather hinges, and fastened by a wooden button. Such a cabinet, neatly finished, looks very well, and costs almost nothing. To those who would like to try their hands at something a little more elegant, we offer the following simple design :

The picture shows the cabinet complete, and the plan following it is drawn so that every measurement in it is one-sixteenth of the corresponding measurement in the finished cabinet. No nails are used. Wood of light color looks well; chestnut is easily worked. The ends of the top and bottom are mortised into the sides. Close to the side boards, holes are bored

through the projecting parts of the tenons; and wedges are inserted and hammered tight.

The frames of the doors are doweled at the corners, each joint being made by boring a hole through one piece into the next, and inserting a dowel coated with glue. The short dotted lines in the plan help to explain this. The glass should not be set with putty, but with narrow strips, beading, or rattan, fastened with brads or needle-points. Butt-hinges may be used, with ornamental hinge-plates set outside as shown. Hook one door to the shelf, and it will hold the other door shut.

The shelves may be made with raised edges, like trays—the front rims are not shown in the picture on the following page. These edges will keep the contents from rolling off when the trays are taken out. The shelves slope forward to show the specimens to better advantage; and they rest on dowels let into auger-holes in the side boards. To prevent them from slipping, pegs are set in them underneath, resting against the backs of the forward dowels. The shelves may be put in flat, and may rest on screw-eyes screwed into the sides of the cabinet.

Metal ears are set on the back, projecting above the top, for hanging the cabinet ; in addition, it is well to drive a screw from the inside through the back into a stud in the wall.

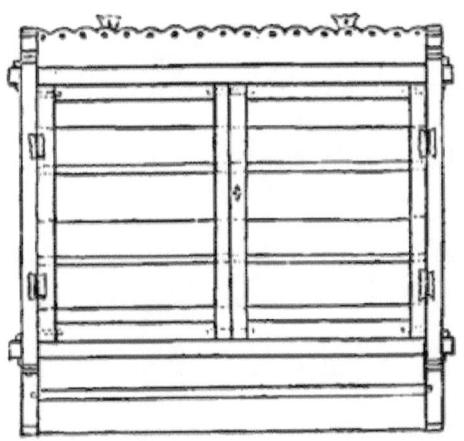

The scalloping at the top of the back may be done with a fret-saw. The hole in the center of each scallop is bored right through. The ornamental lines across the sides are made with a gouge, and should be covered with two coats of white shellac varnish. Those skilled in fret-sawing may like to set in the top the letters **A. A.**, in Old English text. If you are puzzled over any of the details, the nearest cabinet-maker will give you a friendly hint.

Many chapters, wishing something still more elaborate, have given various sorts of entertainments, and earned money to buy them, and in many cases the school authorities have generously furnished our young friends with cabinets, and rendered them other substantial aid.

One of the most desirable kinds of cabinet is made like a shallow show-case, and the top is covered with a glass door which may be lifted up. In a case for insects, this top may be tightly fastened down by means of thumb-screws, and may be rendered airtight by the interposition of strips of rubber.

CHAPTER V.

THE COLLECTION OF PLANTS.

A FEW words may be useful in regard to the collection and preservation of plants. The processes are simple and easily learned, yet it is astonishing how few seem to acquire them. Things are sent to a botanist for identification in such form as to make him shiver, devoid of essential parts, ill selected, and badly, or not at all, pressed. Good judgment lies at the bottom of specimen-making—as it does of most other things. We may lay down rules in vain if common sense comes not in to temper and control. There is no rule for supplying this ; it is a matter of temperament and antecedents, though it may be increased by education. A sense of neatness is almost as essential.

Now as to directions. First, when you go on an excursion, wear strong and plain clothes that you are not fearful of injuring. Briers and bogs are no respecters of raiment. Select broad, low-heeled, comfortable shoes. Repentance follows upon a tight boot, especially in mountainous regions. And, by the way, in such rough districts, it is well to stud the soles with hob-nails. They aid very much in climbing.

The outfit should consist of a pocket-knife of some sort, a cane, hooked at the end, for pulling down branches of trees, or securing water-plants otherwise unattainable ; a ball of twine ; some vials and pill-boxes. The last are carried, not for any medicinal value, but for preserving seeds, algæ or other small objects.

By all means take a note-book in which to jot down memoranda of various sorts. Few persons can trust the memory implicitly concerning the occupations and collections of a day. Field-notes carefully made are often of more value to others than to the person immediately concerned. Moreover, the taking of them inculcates a useful lesson of painstaking observation, terse expression, and neatness of style. Nothing should be done in a slovenly way. Sketches, well made, and illustrative either of landscapes or plants, are a commendable addition to such notes. A set of such note-books, kept through a series of years, becomes, indeed, a diary of delightful facts. Throughout life, and in periods of despondency, the records will recall scenes of inexpressible joy. It is well to provide one's self with a pocket-map of the county or region to be visited. On this can be recorded the roads, forests, hills, springs, marshes, etc. The geological formation, too, can be put in by colors, and even the favorite haunts of the rarer flowers can be indicated.

It is surprising how, by this means, a person will acquire a nearly perfect knowledge of the features of a district. If your state or county is a large one, cut up the map into portions, and paste these on cloth.

If you have an eye to the inner man and creature-comforts, take a drinking-cup and provide a luncheon. In these preliminary directions we have cleared the way for the consideration of the really technical apparatus required. There are two modes of collecting plants, both of which possess certain advantages. We find different collectors wedded to one or the other, and, indeed, prepared to do valorous battle for the one they have chosen. Our own attitude is conservative. Sometimes we try one place, sometimes another. It depends somewhat upon the occasion and the environment. Some botanists use only the tin box; others use only the portfolio. We employ either or both as the case demands. The box, or *vasculum*, is usually a flattened cylinder of any size to suit the caprice of the owner.

It opens through nearly the whole of one side, and has a cover confined by a sliding bar. We have one small one, and another that is often mistaken for a wash-boiler. Such a box may be of one compartment, or divided into several. Plants, especially if closely packed, will keep in it for a long time. For ordinary study or school work, the box is to be preferred. By it the plants are brought in fresh, and with their natural contour and expression. It is well during a journey to sprinkle them with water now and then. Probably the largest and best collections are made by means of the portfolio. This consists essentially of two binder's-boards of standard size, 17 x 12 in.—that is, a little larger than the sheets upon which the plants are subsequently to be mounted. These should be covered with enameled cloth, and left free; that is, not connected by the back in the manner of a book. Around them must pass a couple of straps, held in place, and by which pressure can be brought to bear on the contained papers. Within these covers we have the field-folios, or sheets of bibulous paper, with here and there a regular drier to give firmness to the whole. So much for outfit. We must now state how our apparatus is to be used. The first thing is to select your plants. Beginners make the mistake of collecting things that are too young—perhaps with a fellow-feeling for the inexperienced. Be patient! Wait till the plants are well in flower, and if possible, even partly in fruit. If you cannot get fruit and flower together, visit the locality again for the former. At any rate, *always secure it.* The fruit is often essential to the identification of a plant. In the same way one must have the underground parts, roots, tubers, root-stocks, etc., paring these down if too bulky. Do not, on any account, merely nip off the top of a plant, and think you have a specimen. You will, in such case, only lay up trouble for yourself and others.

Ferns require the underground parts. The *Umbelliferæ, Cruciferæ, Carices,* and *Potamogetons must* be collected in fruit. Grasses, on the other hand, oftener need the flowers.

Generally a number of specimens will be growing together. Of these some will be better than others. Select the best; those which seem most representative, least injured in any way; good average examples of the whole. If you are using the box, no special advice is necessary. Lay the plants in smoothly, avoiding injury so far as is possible. If the portfolio is employed, open it, and put one or more plants of the *same species* in a single sheet, carefully laying them out, and then bringing down the upper sheet over them. On either side put drying-papers, then another species-sheet with more specimens, then more driers, and so on. Never mix species on the same sheet. Put with each species a field-label, stating, if known, the name of the plant, and the date and place of collection. To these data may usefully be added color of flower, height of plant, nature of soil, and habit of growth, though much of such information is best left in the note-book, with reference to the specimens.

The ultimate process of drying, upon which so much depends, is, in effect, pretty much the same as the field-work with the portfolio, only now one uses a regular press. We say a *regular* one ; but, on second thought, we should correct by saying the simplest press you can make. As good as any consists of two strong, cleated boards, with a weight on top. The plants are removed from box or portfolio, and placed *in their species-sheets*, between driers, or wads of bibulous paper. A pile is thus made. The specimens remain permanently in their special folios, but the driers must be frequently changed, and new ones put in, while the wet ones are exposed to sunlight or heat. Herein is the whole secret of good specimen-making : *well-regulated pressure*, and *incessant change of driers.*

We ought to state, however, as this is a perverse world, and inanimate objects often seem imp-directed, that when one wholly forgets a series of specimens, and leaves them in the press for weeks, they occasionally come out better than others that have been watched. Yet, dear youthful collector, build not too high hope on this result of laziness! Eternal vigilance is the rule. Various forms of press are used. Some are provided with straps, others with screws and levers. After all, a simple weight, following the plants down as they shrink, is as good as any thing. The length of time that a plant should remain in press can best be learned from experience. Judge by the feeling whether it is dry. If still damp, let it remain.

THE MOUNTING OF PLANTS.

The collector's work does not cease when he has pressed his plants. Indeed, it has then hardly begun. Supposing that they are now perfectly dried, they must next be poisoned. This is necessary to prevent the attacks of insects which will otherwise be likely completely to destroy them. One has a feeling of despair when he goes to his cases some day and finds the work of years in ruins. Corrosive sublimate applied with a soft brush is the best remedy known. It should be dissolved almost to saturation in strong alcohol, and the bottle plainly marked as poisonous. Keep the solution out of the way of small children and irresponsible persons. Small plants may be directly immersed in the fluid, contained for the time in a shallow pan.

Prevention is better than cure. Keep the bugs out in the first place. Cases cannot be too tight. Mr. Sereno Watson tells us that he would rather rely on a tight case than on the poison itself. Inquire always whether plants received in exchange have been properly poisoned. Quarantine them until you are sure. If, despite all precautions, the cases become infested, fumigate them with bisulphide of carbon. Here, again, bear in mind that this liquid is dangerously inflammable. Put a little of it in each case. In a few hours it will evaporate. Then open windows and ventilate the room before bringing lights, or fire of any kind, near.

Plants are mounted in various ways according to individual taste and judgment. Sometimes they are stuck down by slips of adhesive paper; oftener by glue. We ourselves employ Le Page's carriage-glue, and thus escape the nuisance of a glue-pot. The medium is always ready. Apply the glue lightly on one side of the plant, laid for the time on a sheet of waste paper. Then lay the plant, sticky side down, on the sheet to which it is to be fixed. Place over it some drying paper, and apply light pressure. We often mount a hundred plants in a day. Put only one species on a sheet. In order to make your heap lie smooth in the case, and without bulging in the middle, place some plants on one margin of the page; others on the opposite margin; some at the top, others at

the bottom. Leave room, if you can, for other specimens of the same plant from other places. Apply
your own label to the lower right-hand side ; the collector's label to the lower left. On these labels write
legibly the name of the plant, the date and place of
collection, and such other data as can be compressed
in so limited space. A portion of the label can
always be printed as per sample :

HERBARIUM OF T. Z. JONES.

Much bad taste is shown in the construction of
labels. Avoid all tendency to fancy borders. Strive
for clearness and simplicity. At the same time, let
the paper of the label be such as will readily take glue
without too much curling. Mounting-paper can be
obtained from any naturalists' agency, or from a bind-
ery. The standard size is 16½ inches by 11½. Uni-
formity is desirable, so that when the collection is
broken up, as it is sure to be in time, it may find a
fitting abode in some public herbarium.

Our plants are now mounted and labeled. Place
them next under their proper 'genus covers,' and in
their ordinal relations in the proper pigeon-holes of
your case. It would lead us too far to speak of the
various cases used. Suffice it to say that the case
should be of convenient height, and the compartments
deep and broad enough easily to receive the sheets.
If possible have tight doors, excluding dust and insects—the whole fastening by the ' Jenks,' or some
other combination lock.

We are often asked how to learn classification. It
can be learned only by classifying. A summer spent

in collecting and arranging a lot of plants conveys more definite ideas of 'affinity' than hours of lecturing. It is the fashion nowadays to decry systematic work, but it is likely to have its uses for some time to come. The average young pupil is more interested in the plants afield than in the differentiation of the *punctum vegetationis :* at least such is our experience.

In conclusion, we will say that dried plants can be studied almost as well as the fresh. A short soaking in water softens the parts, restores the contours, and makes everything available for dissection. Indeed, the larger part of a systematic botanist's work is upon dried plants. The herbarium is a sort of cyclopædia —a book of reference, where the explanations are afforded by the plants themselves. It is out of the question personally to collect all the plants even of a single family whose times of blooming and fruiting are different, and whose localities are remote, and perhaps to you inaccessible. In the herbarium you have the whole range side by side and can institute comparisons. In the useful study of plant-distribution, as in many other ways, then, the *hortus siccus* is a necessity.

It may not be out of place, in connection with rules for preserving plants, to give the following method of preparing specimens of wood for the cabinet : Cut boards five by eight inches and a quarter of an inch thick. Season, and plane smooth. Varnish one-half. Then cut from a sapling, two or three inches in diameter, some pieces one-quarter of an inch thick. Saw these in a square mitre-box. Saw off several, as some may warp or split. In summer, the pieces will season without a fire. In winter, a fire is needed, but the wood should not be put too near it. When the end sections are seasoned, smooth one side carefully with a rasp, so as not to mar the bark. Finish with fine sand-paper.

Polish, oil, or varnish, being careful not to varnish the bark. When dry, fasten with small screws, from the back, to the centre of the boards previously described.

For most of the excellent advice regarding the care of plants, which is presented in this chapter, we are indebted to Prof. W. Whitman Bailey, who gave it first in *The Swiss Cross.* In closing, we commend to our readers the following hints contained in a letter from Mr. Herbert M. Ellis to the Selborne Society of England:

"It seems most curious, and yet I think there can be no doubt of the fact, that the chief culprits as re-

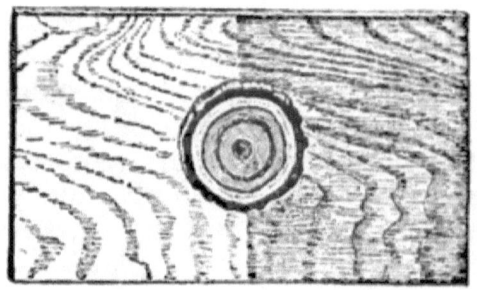

SPECIMEN OF WOOD.

gards the destruction of wild flowers and ferns, and birds and insects, are those who in their hearts have most sympathy and love for them. One of those benighted beings, though I suppose they form the majority of our fellow-creatures, on whom the quiet beauty and serene loveliness of the country is lost, to whom a growing field in June is but a field of grass, to whom the loveliest dell in Devonshire is only worthy of notice if he wants a quiet smoke, whose only manner of distinction among birds is large or small, to whom all sea-birds are gulls, all water-birds dabchicks, and all wild flowers simply as the grass under his feet—such

a one, though much to be pitied, is quite innocent of
the posies of dead wild flowers by the wayside, or the
ghastly arrays of ill-stuffed birds and beasts in musty
cupboards and on bookshelves at home, or heaps of
unfortunate little butterflies which never get as far as
the setting-board.   No ; such sights as these are generally the work of those who love the things of nature
not wisely, but too well.   Like Mother Eve, they cannot be satisfied with seeing, without wanting to possess
more than is necessary for them or good for others.
What is it, then, that is needed in our rambles and excursions ?   Is it not a thoughtful love for these things ?
I would offer the following practical suggestions, which
I think can scarcely hinder any one from enjoying the
country as much as ever, and at the same time help to
carry out the objects which your Society has in view :

1. When in the country do not ruthlessly pull up
and pick every flower you come across when you first
set off.   Gather your flowers if possible in the latter
part of the day, when they will be less likely to die.

2. Do not entirely denude one place of flowers,
whatever they may be.

3. Do not pluck flowers which by nature fade directly, such as wood anemones and wood sorrel, which
never look half so well in vases as in their native
place.

4. Do not dig up flower-roots at the time of flowering, a most common and pernicious practice ; it is the
worst possible time for transplanting."

CHAPTER VI.

HOW TO COLLECT AND PRESERVE SEA-WEED.

LOUISA LANE CLARKE, in 'Common Sea-weeds,' gives the following suggestions, which are evidently the fruit of experience: " We dabble in the cool, clear tide-pools, and scarcely know what we take up; there is a world of life in each. The speckled prawn is balancing himself, and waving to and fro his sensitive feelers, springing away under the rich foliage that conceals his hiding-place; and the small blenny darts like a lightning-flash from cranny to crevice, the fear and the dread of man upon it. On the green *Ulva* creeps the lovely little slug—a bright green, spotted with white—called *Acteon viridis*, and on darker sea-weeds the great purplish sea-hare. Sea-spiders lurk amid the coralline; and as we gather a bunch of sea-weed, we shake out dozens of a pretty little snail called *Rissoa*, besides gathering, if we please, bright yellow *Nerita*, the commonest sea-snail of our coast. All these force themselves on the notice of the sea-weed gatherer, as we scramble over the rocks, and pause to consider where we shall begin.

I advise taking a little of everything—not much, for they so soon spoil in waiting to be mounted—and naming each specimen as it is decided by reference to your manual. If you have but a day for a sea-side holiday, go down to the lowest ebb of the tide, in hopes of the best *red* sea-weeds, and work back to the commoner, but still beautiful, green sea-weeds, *Ulva* and *Cladophoræ*.

Suppose, now, that we have made our search, and have brought home a tangled mass of olive, red, and green sea-weeds.

We get some soup-plates, fresh water, a bit of alum, some camel-hair pencils, and *I* use needles mounted on lucifer matches, to assist in disentangling the mass.

Of course we are prepared with paper cut into large and small squares ; and, as much of the beauty of the specimens depends on the quality of the paper, it should be fine, and at the same time stout, almost as good as drawing-paper.

Now float a piece of weed in fresh water ; if very dirty or sandy, wash it first, and in renewed water float it on a piece of paper supported by your left hand, whilst with your right hand you arrange the plant in a natural manner, using a mounted needle or porcupine-quill, and thinning out the superabundant branches with a fine-pointed pair of scissors. When the specimen is placed as you like it, cautiously raise the paper that the position of the plant be not altered, and let it rest somewhere with sloping inclination, that the moisture may run off whilst other specimens are treated in the same way.

Do not leave them long thus, for they must be pressed before the paper is dry.

A convenient traveling-press consists of two pieces of deal board about two feet long and one foot wide, a couple of quires of whity-brown paper, and a double strap. Lay blotting-paper between the coarser paper, and you can strap them closely and carry your seaweed very safely in your hand.

In drying them, you must have old linen or fine muslin, old and soft, to lay upon the weed and prevent it sticking to the upper paper, but do not leave it beyond a day or so, lest it leave chequered marks upon the surface of the weed, especially those with broad fronds, like *Delesseria*.

Experience will give the best lessons. Some sea-weeds, such as *Melogloia*, which are glutinous, must not be pressed at all, but laid out to dry, and when perfectly so, then moisten the *under* side of the paper, and give a gentle pressure only.

Others will not adhere to paper, and therefore, when dry, brush them over with a little isinglass dissolved in gin (laid on warm), and they will then be fixed closely to the card-board or paper.

Another preparation is : One ounce oil of turpentine, in which some gum mastic the size of a nutmeg has been dissolved. This gives a gloss to the specimen, and helps to preserve the color.

You must change the blotting-paper and muslin at least twice during the process of drying larger seaweeds ; the smaller ones will be ready in a couple of days for the album, on the second day giving heavy pressure by stones and weights besides the strap.

CHAPTER VII.

PLANS FOR BOTANICAL WORK.

THE following suggestions written by Mr. Wm. B. Werthner, for Chapter 940, Dayton, O., are so exceedingly practical and valuable that we are glad to reproduce them here for the benefit of the whole Association :

" As spring comes on, an interest in nature is awakened, and as botany offers so many fields for individual work, the following suggestions are made with the hope that they may induce more out-of-door study. The student will easily find that one season's work does not exhaust the subject, and that he may continue from year to year, always learning some things he did not know before, and that his investigations may lead to discoveries of the highest importance, giving him a deeper understanding of natural forces and a better appreciation of life itself. This science is so comprehensive that men have long ago given up the idea of being master of it all ; and so you will see that one or two things carefully studied and collected will give you more pleasure, and lead to better results, than a superficial study of the whole field.

The question is asked : What can I do out of school, in summer and other times, to keep up my interest or direct my attention to botanical problems ? Here are a few topics for investigation :

I. Make *experiments* with living plants.

    (*a*) *Seedlings*. Note under what circumstances different seeds will germinate ; whether they all need the same amounts of air, warmth, water, etc. Compare their modes of growth ; plant in various kinds of soil, and at different times.

(*b*) Make a study of the *life history* of a single plant ; start corn, beans, peas, sunflowers, morning-glories, etc., to growing ; study the needs and behavior of the growing plant, its rapidity of growth, its relation to warmth, light, water, wind, insects, other plants ; learn the uses of all its parts ; note the circumstances of the unfolding of its buds, leaves, flowers, the formation of its fruit ; watch it daily and write down your observations ; draw all its organs ; investigate its motions and determine their causes and uses. You will often be in the dark about certain phenomena, but the work will be of great interest.

(*c*) *Cut off parts,* such as branches, flowers, leaves ; keep them in water and watch closely ; plant them to see if they will take root.

(*d*) Subject certain plants to various amounts of *light, heat* or *water;* note their behavior.

(*e*) Make special study of the *movements* of plants ; of what use they are ; how caused ; observe the conditions under which blossoms open and close, or leaves turn, or tendrils curl, etc.

II. *Habitats* of plants ; why some grow here and not there ; why some are very common and others restricted to very narrow limits ; what effect a certain location may have on the plant.

III. Collect and study certain *families* or groups, such as violets, roses, cresses, mints, grasses, composites, ferns, mosses, etc. See why they are grouped together, what ties of relationship they have, whether of size, structure, habitat ; whether certain families are more common in some places than others, and why?

IV. *Local Flora,* the plants of a certain locality, a wood, meadow, railroad-bank, swamp, etc. Follow up a brook, find what plants accompany it, why they are absent in some places and abundant in others. A waste piece of land; see what weeds, shrubs or trees are there; how they came, which were first arrivals, why not all the immigrants remained. Or try to account for the large number of plants often found crowned in the same field.

V. Plants found growing without cultivation within the *city limits;* account for their presence; note whether they are transient, or appear from year to year.

VI. Make a study of the many *parasites* found on plants. (With these microscopes should be used).

VII. Make *comparative* studies of buds, roots, leaves, bark, leaf-scars, pith, etc.; get many specimens to compare form, size, structure; see how similar functions are performed in very different ways, or how similar organs have very different offices; *e. g.,* see how climbing may be accomplished in one plant by twining, in another by tendrils, a third by rootlets, a fourth by hooks, etc., or learn how one tree may have its buds protected by scales, another by wool, a third by varnish, etc.

VIII. Collect and study different kinds of *wood;* quality, color, uses, structure, etc. Make sections and study with the microscope; note the difference between heart wood and sap wood, or between roots and branches, or the nature of woody climbing plants.

IX. Make *drawing from nature* a specialty; buds and branches, leaves, flowers, fruits, seeds, entire plants.

X. *Trees;* their appearance in winter and in summer; their foliage, mode of branching, habitats, etc. Note localities where fine specimens occur, take measures; learn to distinguish them by their bark, branches, leaves, as well as flowers and fruits. Take a single tree, *e. g.*, the hickory, for special investigation ; collect and study its buds, branches, bark, wood, leaves, flowers, nuts, seedlings, saplings, etc. Learn the uses of forests, their relations to rivers, winds, frosts, rain ; their help to civilization, the desirability of trees and parks in cities.

XI. *Fruits* and *seeds;* color, form, structure, modes of attachment ; make sections and draw. Study the *distribution* of plants, the agencies concerned (such as insects, birds, squirrels, other animals, wind, rivers, etc.) ; see how man voluntarily and otherwise aids in this process. Note the various adaptations in fruits, seeds, or in the whole plant to further dissemination.

XII. *Color in plants.*

(1) Of flowers ; note whether the seasons have particularly prominent colors ; whether the colors have any relation to insects ; make lists of white flowers, of red, yellow, blue, etc.

(2) Of fruits ; aids to dispersion by birds, protective colors of green fruits, etc.

(3) Of foliage ; relation to the season, light, shade, etc.

XIII. Our *native shrubs;* collect and study the flowers and fruits ; note their habitats.

XIV. Make lists of *spring flowers*, summer flowers, etc., or flowers of a certain month. Note the procession of flowers.

XV. Study the *odors* of flowers ; make lists of fragrant ones, note at what seasons they are found, and their relation to the color, habitat, etc., of the plant, and to insects.

XVI. Study the *weeds* of a locality, and try to learn. why they are so common, how their seeds are carried, why they are troublesome or so difficult to exterminate. Try to find out their original home by reference to books.

XVII. Make a list of the *flowering times* of our commonest plants. Repeat this next year and note whether the dates are the same ; if not, why ?

XVIII. Note the ways in which plants *protect* themselves against cold, rain, insects, or other enemies ; study thorns, prickles, hairs, wax, bad odors, etc.

XIX. Relations of plants *to each other ;* helpful, harmful.

XX. Relations of *animals to plants ;* helpful in distributing seeds or carrying pollen ; harmful in destroying leaves, buds, fruits, roots, etc.

XXI. Relation of *wind* and *water* to plants ; carrying pollen, seed, roots, etc. Wind bringing rain, rain dissolving food in ground, etc.

XXII. *Climbing plants ;* make list of those found ; study their ways and means and habitats ; note how the same end may be attained in very different manners ; observe how trees and other objects on which they grow are affected.

XXIII. Study those plants that bloom *before their leaves appear ;* those whose flowers and leaves appear together ; try to understand the advantages of such habits.

XXIV. See why *insects* visit flowers, how they are attracted, of what use they are to the plant, and what various mutual adaptations have taken place. Note whether insects visit only certain flowers, or any indiscriminately ; find out whether they can distinguish colors or the fragrance of blossoms. Note how *cross-fertilization* is also carried on in other ways, by wind, birds, etc.

XXV. Study the *phyllotaxy*, not alone of trees, but also of shrubs and herbs, as well as flower-clusters and fruits. Those who take pleasure in mathematical problems will find some here in Nature's workshop that will give them plenty to do. Make lists of your findings.

XXVI. *Monœcious* and *Diœcious* plants; make lists; note their places of growth, how far the latter are often apart, and by what means the pollen is carried.

XXVII. *Winged fruits.*

XXVIII. Plants *injurious to man.*

XXIX. *Aquatic plants;* foliage, time and manner of flowering, etc.

XXX. Effects of *cultivation* on plants.

XXXI. Watch the *development of the fruit* from the flower through its various stages in the cherry, apple, rose, grape, maple, pea, bean, walnut, corn, etc.

The most enjoyable and profitable way of studying or collecting is that of *personal* search and independent work.

Look for specimens on all your walks, keep your eyes open ; you have no idea how much your powers of observation will be increased by constant practice.

Never go out without your *tools* — knife, trowel, string, note-book and pencil, and whatever you may want to use in carrying home your specimens. Don't be satisfied with the observations merely ; *write* down what you have seen, note any questions that may occur to you, for future study.

Always *date* your finds, giving time, place, and circumstance ; otherwise your observations will too often be useless. Repeat your work, and don't be in a hurry. Nature herself is not.

Make frequent *drawings*, not so much that you may become proficient in this art (though this would be great gain), but that you may see the parts of the object clearly and make them your own.

CHAPTER VIII.

Of the members of the Agassiz Association, more have expressed a preference for the study of entomology than for almost any other branch. Curiously enough, the girls seem to be quite as fond of insects as the boys are. It is not difficult to account for this preference. The many-hued wings of butterflies flashing in the sun, the metallic gleam of beetles, the feathery grace and rich coloring of the moths, the dreamy pinions of dragon-flies, the excitement of the chase, and above all, the mysterious and symbolic changes which attend insect life, shed a bright fascination about insect-study.

Attracted by this light our boys and girls are fluttering about the homes of bugs and beetles very much in the same manner that bugs and beetles flutter about the lights in our human habitations. Let me, then, hasten to answer the three questions which are puzzling so many of our correspondents : How catch? how kill? how keep? By far the best way to catch a butterfly is to find a caterpillar ; keep him in a glass box ; feed him with leaves of the plant on which you found him ; and watch him day by day, as he changes his various garments, spins himself up till he bursts or perforates his cerements and unrolls his wings, with every painted shingle in its place, his feathers quite unruffled on his head, and his six legs under him in unmutilated perfection.

In addition to this method of capture, you will need a light gauze net. Any boy can make one of these in half an hour. Get three-fourths of a yard of silk veiling; ask mother to make a bag of it, with a hem around the top wide enough to run a pipe-stem through; pass a thick wire through this, and bend it into the shape required; fasten the ends of this wire to a light stick, five or six feet long, and your net is made. A piece of a bamboo fishing-rod makes a good handle. You may also need a stouter net for beating about in the bushes.

A third method of capturing moths is that of painting trees with a mixture of rum, beer, and sugar. This is done in the early evening, and later, lantern in hand, you go about from tree to tree and tap into your net the insects stupefied by the sweet but fatal sirup.

A very successful lure may be formed by enclosing a female moth, alive, in a box covered with gauze. Frequently a large number of moths may be taken in a single evening as they hover about the imprisoned insect.

For the capture and conveyance of beetles, etc., a good supply of pill-boxes and vials of various sizes may be carried in the pockets. Small forceps are convenient for picking up spiders, which, however, are not now classed with true insects.

These smaller insects may be dropped at once into a bottle of alcohol, and cared for on reaching home.

Butterflies are easily killed by a sudden and strong compression of the thorax. They are best carried home by folding the wings back and enclosing them in little three-cornered envelopes, not glued, but merely folded over them.

A vial of chloroform with a camel's-hair brush attached to the inside of its rubber cork, is convenient. A drop on the head of an insect will render it insensible, and it may be pinned into your collecting-box. But the best means for killing large insects is the *cyanide-jar*.

Take a wide-mouthed candy-jar; get your druggist to lay four or five pieces of cyanide of potassium as large as walnuts in it, and cover them with a layer of sawdust. Over this fit a piece of writing-paper. Then pour over all half an inch of liquid plaster-of-Paris. This will quickly harden, forming a smooth floor, on which any insect when dropped, will quickly and quietly die.

The jar must be labeled poison, and must be kept closed with an air-tight cover.

A collecting-case can be made of any light, shallow box, by lining it with cork, and affixing straps by which it may be slung around the neck. Compartments may be made in it, for the cyanide and chloroform bottles, for forceps, insect-pins, envelopes, etc. Having got your insects home, they must be carefully mounted. You should have several 'setting-boards.' These are simply thin boards, grooved at intervals so as to admit the bodies of moths and butterflies, in such a way that their wings may be flat on the board. Strips of cork may be glued along the bottom of the grooves to receive the pins.

Pin your specimens in a groove of proper depth, and spread the wings carefully with your forceps, or with needles set in wooden handles.

Fasten them by laying strips of glass over them, or by pinning strips of paper across them. They should be allowed to dry for a week or two according to size. The bodies of large lepidoptera should be brushed with a solution of corrosive sublimate, one-half drachm; arsenic, four grains; alcohol, one-half pint. This is, of course, very poisonous, and should be so labeled and treated.

If your insects have become dry and brittle, they must be relaxed before you attempt to mount them. This may be done by laying them on wet sand, but

Mr. Neumogen, who has one of the largest collections in the world, places such specimens in a small tin box provided with a cork bottom. The cork is dampened, and the temperature and moisture is controlled by a pipe that connects the interior of the box with the outside air. In four weeks the most hardened specimen has never failed to relax.

Your insects may now be pinned into cedar cases, made air-tight, and guarded by lumps of camphor gum. In addition to these precautions, all specimens should be subjected to a rigid quarantine of a month before being transferred to the collection. Even then the cases must be carefully examined every month, and any indications of danger must be regarded. If such appear, pour a few drops of chloroform into the case, and close the cover. This will drive the destructive creatures into sight from crack and cranny. Kill them, preserving one or two for specimens, and renew your previous precautions. A simpler, and as effectual a method, is to give your mounted insects, cases and all, a thorough baking in the oven, but this also requires great care, as the heat will spoil some kinds.

Mr. E. S. Morse gives a good device for arranging an insect-box for the cabinet. It consists of a light wooden frame like a slate-frame, with paper stretched upon the upper and lower surfaces. Dampen the paper and glue it to the frame, and when the paper dries, it will contract and become as tight as a drum-head. Inside the box, upon two sides, fasten cleats, and let their top edges be about a quarter of an inch above the bottom. Rest the paper-covered frame upon these cleats. The bottom of the box should be covered with soft pine to receive the points of the pins. The space under the frame should be dusted with snuff and camphor to keep out insects.

But, after having tried many methods, I have been best pleased with the appearance of insects that I have set up on separate papered blocks of wood, such as are used for minerals. Indeed, I know of no way of showing any of the smaller specimens, such as shells, bird's-eggs, insects, and fossils, to so good advantage as to set each by itself on a white block of suitable size.

I will add for the benefit of our young entomologists a few hints on methods of observation furnished by Prof. G. Howard Parker, of Cambridge, and Prof. Asa Packard, Jr., of Providence. Every naturalist should have a pocket note-book always with him, and make careful entries of such points as are here indicated. Suppose, for example, you take first, butterflies and moths. It would be an excellent plan to prepare a paper, in which you might :

1. Give a brief but clear description of the *order* (*Lepidoptera*).

2. Give a careful report of your own observations on any one species of the order. In this report should be included :

A. *Description* of the insect, accurate as may be, and, if possible, accompanied by drawings, however rude.

[This description should be made as follows :

a. If a moth or butterfly, note : 1st. The *form of the antennæ*, whether pectinated or simply hairy, or spindle-shaped. 2d. The form and size of palpi. and length of tongue. 3d. Wings : First pair, form, shape of costal, apex, outer-edge veins. Second pair, same. 4th. Markings on wings. 5th. Feet, spurs.

b. If a caterpillar, note : 1st. Form of head, wider or narrower than segment next. 2d. Dorsal, subdorsal, and lateral stripes. 3d. Position of tubercles, warts or spines, and spots. 4th. Spiracular line. 5th. Supra-anal plate ; its form and markings. 6th. Number of abdominal legs, and form of last pair.

c. Difference in coloration of the sexes ; varieties observed ; probable cause of such variation, such as differences of food, location, and time of year.]

B. *Habits.*—Date of appearance and disappearance of the *perfect insect;* number of annual broods; localities most favorable, etc.

C. *Transformations.*—1. The egg : description, sketch, duration of this stage ; where and how deposited by the female. 2. Larva : number of molts, and changes noticed in these molts ; duration of each molt, and entire time consumed in this stage ; food-plants of the larva ; drawings. 3. Chrysalis : description ; methods of protection and fastening ; duration of this stage ; special observations. 4. Parasites observed during these stages (ichneumons, chalcids, etc.).

D. Concluding remarks, with notes drawn from various works on the subject, and a list of such references.

Having thus worked up a few species of *Lepidoptera*, you might, to advantage, take up successively the other orders, *Hymenoptera*, *Coleoptera*, *Neuroptera*, etc., treating them in the same way, and concluding the course by a careful study of insects as a class. Then you can return to your favorite order or family, and carry on your special researches and observations, minutely and intelligently.

We add the following Department directions for sending insects by mail :

All inquiries about insects, injurious or otherwise, should be accompanied by specimens, the more the better. Such specimens, if dead, should be packed in some soft material, as cotton or wool, and inclosed in some stout tin or wooden box. They will come by mail for one cent per ounce. *Insects should never be inclosed loose in the letter.* Whenever possible, larvæ (*i. e.*, grubs, caterpillars, maggots, etc.) should be packed alive in some tight tin box—the tighter the better, as air-holes are not needed—along with a supply of their appropriate food sufficient to last them on their journey ; otherwise, they generally die on the road and shrivel up. Send as full an account as possible of the habits of the insect respecting which you desire information ; for example, what plant or plants it infests ; whether it destroys the leaves, the buds, the twigs, or the stem ; how long it has been known to you ; what amount of damage it has done, etc. Such particulars are often

not only of high scientific interest, but of great practical importance. In sending soft insects or larvæ that have been killed in
alcohol, they should be packed in cotton saturated with alcohol.
In sending pinned or mounted insects, always pin them securely in
a box to be inclosed in a larger box, the space between the two
boxes to be packed with some soft or elastic material, to prevent
too violent jarring. *Packages should be marked with the name of
the sender.*

In reply to numerous inquiries concerning entomological books, we recommend to the general student
'Harris on Insects Injurious to Vegetation,' and
Packard's 'Guide to the Study of Insects;' and to
those beginning the study, 'Insect Lives,' published
at one dollar by The Writers Publishing Company, of
New York. The last is the only book of low price we
know of that treats the subject so as to make it interesting to the young.

CHAPTER IX.

HOW TO COLLECT AND PRESERVE BIRDS AND EGGS.

It is hardly worth while to make a collection of mounted birds. This requires too much time and too much room. But, especially, skins are better and more convenient for study than mounted birds. Skins may be kept in a cabinet with tightly fitting drawers, with plenty of camphor, or insect-powder. The best arm for general purposes is the double-barreled, breech-loading shot-gun. Three-fourths of your cartridges should contain small charges of mustard-seed shot, and the remainder, No. 8 and No. 4. You can indicate the kind of shot in each shell by having numbers on your shot-wads. Early morning and late evening are the best hours, and well-watered and wooded spots among the best places for collecting; although, as each bird has its own peculiar haunts, the hunter should cover as wide a range, and as great a variety of country, as possible. As each specimen is secured, it must be carefully cleansed and smoothed. Plug mouth, nostrils, vent, and shot-holes with cotton, and thrust the bird head-first into a paper cone, to keep the plumage from injury.

A fish-basket is excellent to carry the birds home. Before skinning, each bird should be measured, to determine the total length, and the spread of wings. Note, also, the color of the eyes, bill, and feet, as they may fade. Enter all these memoranda in a note-book, and also on the specimen label. Add also date of capture, sex, locality, name of collector, etc.

SKINNING.

We do not propose here to attempt a detailed account of the taxidermist's art, but the general mode of procedure should be as follows :

See that throat, nostrils, and wounds are well plugged with cotton, and fasten some also around the bill. Should any blood get on the feathers, remove it at once with a damp sponge, and dry with plaster-of-Paris. Lay the bird on its back, separate the breast-feathers right and left, cut from the breast-bone to the vent (not cutting the flesh), and raise the skin carefully on each side as far as the legs. Cut off the legs at the knee-joints, inside the skin, and afterward skin down to the tarsus, scraping the flesh from the shin-bone, but leaving that bone in place. Next skin around the coccyx, or tail-bones, and cut off the coccyx inside the skin, leaving enough flesh to hold the feathers.

Large birds can often be more easily handled if suspended, head downward before the operator, by a strong hook firmly inserted in the exposed stump of the rump ; but with a little experience this becomes unnecessary. Now carefully strip off the skin, turning it back like a glove, as far as the wings ; cut off the wings, inside the skin, at shoulder-joint. Skin the wing-bones and scrape the flesh from them, as from the legs. Skin over the head to the bill, taking especial care not to stretch the skin. The skin above the ears and eyes will have to be detached by cutting. The eyes must now be picked out, and the entire base of the skull removed, together with the brain, and the flesh between the jaws. If the head is too large to be skinned in this way, some persons make an incision under the throat, but a writer in *Random Notes* gives the better method of opening it on the back of the head.

The skin is now inside out. Powder with arsenic, or soap with arsenic soap, turn it right side out, smooth the plumage, set the bones of legs and wings into proper position, and the bird is ready for stuffing. A pellet of cotton, as large as the bird's eye, should be passed into the skin, and pressed into each socket. Over this adjust the eyelids. Wrap a little cotton around the leg-bones of large birds. Insert a cylinder of cotton, rather smaller than the neck, into the neck. Mould the body-stuffing into a mass, rather smaller than the bird's body. Bring the edges of the skin nicely together over this, and the stuffing is completed. Fold the wings neatly, adjust the head and neck, bring the feet together, and press the bird into the proper shape. The usual fault is too much stuffing, especially between the shoulders. For mounting specimens some knowledge of comparative anatomy is desirable. The habits of each bird must be carefully studied, as well as its peculiar manner of sitting, standing, holding the head, etc. The art of taxidermy should be carefully studied, from such manuals as Swainson's, Brown's, or Sylvester's. Captain Brown's book is published at $1.50, by G. P. Putnam's Sons, of New York. It is still better to secure a few practical lessons from a good taxidermist.

EGG-COLLECTING.

Hardly any other branch of natural history is so liable to abuse as that pertaining to the eggs of birds. There is something fascinating about the search for them. The artful devices of the nest-builders to hide their fragile buildings in sequestered places, as if to challenge the acuteness, alertness, and agility of boys; the interesting structure of the nests; and the rare beauty of the eggs themselves; have always proved stronger temptations to idle plunder than the average youth can resist. Yet great harm is done by an indiscriminate robbery of eggs ; and while oölogy, if scientifically pursued, is an entirely commendable and valuable study, yet we have felt obliged to impose certain not severe restrictions upon its pursuit in connection with our Association. Our attitude is sufficiently defined by the following extract from an editorial note in our official organ, *The Swiss Cross:*

There is no conflict between scientific study and a gentle spirit of mercy. There are, indeed, times when the interests of science require the suffering, and even the death, of insect, bird, and beast ; but every true scientist shrinks from these necessary occasions, and makes them as few as possible. There is no room for cruelty in any laboratory. Whenever pain must be caused, it must be made as slight and as short as it can be made. Whenever life must be taken, it must be taken reverently, as a costly sacrifice, and in the speediest and most merciful manner. The responsibility of drawing the delicate line which is to divide between the cursed ground of cruelty and that honorable but sorrowful region in which the claims of science may properly assume supremacy at the cost of pain, has been forced upon us by the requests of many persons to publish notices of the desired exchange of bird-skins for bird-skins, and of eggs for eggs ; and, on the other hand, by the simultaneous and equally strenuous prayers of well-meaning philozoists, that we would strictly refuse to countenance at all either the killing of birds or the taking of eggs. The solution of the question, which we have reached after long consideration, is included in the following rule, which we shall henceforth adopt, with reference to the publication of such exchange notices :

Notices of the exchange of birds' eggs or bird-skins will be printed in 'The Swiss Cross,' provided that the person sending the notice shall be a member in good standing of the Agassiz Association, that his collections shall have been made in conformity to the laws of the State in which he may reside, and that the description of his material for exchange shall be in terms sufficiently accurate to indicate that he is doing scientific work.

The egg-collector's outfit consists of a pair of climbers, a suit of stout clothing (buttons riveted if possible !), a few tin boxes full of cotton, and a note-book. The best collectors take the nest and a full set of eggs, and in such case they need some sort of basket in which to carry them. Less damage is done by actual students, even if they take the nests and all the eggs, than by mere robbers, who perhaps content themselves with stealing "only one egg from a nest ;" because the latter are never content with one good specimen, but continue pilfering accessible nests until, in some instances, they accumulate hundreds of useless robins' and bluebirds' eggs, and rob the orchards of their melody. Eggs should be blown through one neat hole in the side, and for this purpose a set of egg-drills and a blowpipe should be procured. The specimens should be rinsed with some poisonous solution, and may then be arranged in cabinets in their proper nests, or in compartments filled with sand, cedar sawdust, or cotton. The lesson of their fragility is one speedily learned by experience. It is frequently vividly impressed upon the student while, during his descent from some towering pine or oak, he carries his treasures in that most available receptacle—his mouth.

It may not be out of place to caution the young collector against a danger that attends the exploration of deep holes in trees, such as wrens delight in. Unless the opening is evidently large enough to give comfortable room for the arm, *never allow your arm to crowd into a hole beyond the elbow*, or you may not be able to withdraw it.

With eggs, as with all other specimens, their value depends largely upon the fulness and accuracy of the data accompanying them. Date, location, and description of birds, both male and female, together with such other facts as may be observed, should be carefully noted at the time of collecting, and to this should be added, of course, the name of the collector.

CHAPTER X.

GEOLOGY, the history of the earth, the science of rocks, fossils, and minerals, is the most comprehensive of all the natural sciences, embracing many departments or subordinate sciences, some of which, like mineralogy, are often studied quite independently of the others.

It is unnecessary to refer particularly to the interest and practical importance of this world-wide science; but it is desired to guard the student against discouragement at the outset by calling attention to the fact that, although geology covers so broad a field, and embraces in every department almost endless details, the main principles, and the leading facts, are comparatively few and simple. This is even true in what are often regarded as the dryest branches of geology—descriptive mineralogy and lithology. To acquire a satisfactory and useful knowledge of these subjects is not a vast undertaking; for, although geologists recognize many different species or kinds of minerals and rocks, the most of them are very rare and of little consequence in ordinary life. Not more than twenty minerals, and as many rocks, are of the first importance, but these are very abundant, comprising, so far as we know, at least 999-1000 of the earth.

These few common minerals and rocks are, in one sense, among the most familiar objects of every-day life, for they are in the fields, walls, houses, and streets; and yet how few persons know anything definite about them. There is no other direction in science where so little work will make the student master of so much ground.

It is a great advantage if the study of minerals can be preceded or accompanied by at least a little work in chemistry; and some knowledge of zoology and botany is indispensable to good work in palæontology, or the study of fossils; while other branches of geology make large demands upon physics, mechanics, etc. In short, a competent geologist, in the broadest sense, must be a cultured person in the whole field of natural science.

The golden rule in natural science is to study natural objects rather than books; and it is especially important that this rule should be observed in the study of minerals and rocks. The most perfect descriptions and pictures cannot take the place of the actual specimens or examples, but all knowledge of any real or permanent value must be obtained first hand, *i. e.*, must be based upon personal observation. Books are, of course, useful for reference and to supplement real learning or observation; but the student should regard them merely as auxiliary, and never make them his main reliance.

When we must resort to books, it is, of course, important to have the best; and the list of works relating to the different departments of geology, which may be found on another page, will aid students in making a wise selection.

Since the student's main reliance should be upon nature, and not upon books, the collection of specimens becomes in most cases a very important preliminary to good work in geology. And students and chapters are requested to bear in mind Professor Agassiz's excellent advice to the effect that the most valuable work a society can do, is to make a complete collection and thorough study of the specimens found near its own home. Do not let visions of sparkling crystals or gleaming ores from distant States blind you to the value and importance of the sandstone under your feet, the slate on your roof, the coal in your cellar, or the pebbles by the brook.

Geological collecting is comparatively easy, since minerals and fossils do not have to be pursued over brier and brake, like butterflies, nor are they perishable in their nature. They have not to be pressed nor kept in alcohol. The chief drawback is that rocks are hard and heavy. The former difficulty is, however, readily overcome by a geological hammer, and the latter by a stout bag and a strong arm to carry it, although it is better if the bag can be suspended by a strap from the shoulder.

Hammers of various shapes and sizes are useful in breaking and trimming specimens ; but the best hammer for general use is one weighing from one to two pounds, with a square head at one end, and tapering to a chisel-like edge at the other. The square head is used for breaking and trimming hard masses, while the chisel-edge, which should be at right angles to the handle, is well adapted for splitting shales, schists, etc., and for digging out crystals and fossils. A cold-chisel, or some similar sharp pointed iron, is also very useful for these purposes.

The extraction of fossils from the rock is often an admirable test of patience. If the rock be hard and crystalline, try to get off a chip containing the fossil, take it home, and then with a small (tack) hammer carefully clean it. For the more delicate fossils, like crinoids, various sharp instruments like files or broken dentist's-tools are often useful. Note the essential points in your note-book, and sketch the fossil. If you break it, clean the pieces, and stick them together with mucilage in which a few drops of glycerine have been incorporated. (The glycerine prevents the gum becoming brittle when dry.)

The beautiful ferns, the curious fruits, the ornate *Sigillaria*, and the bewitching glimpse given us of a subtropic jungle, characterizing the coal-formation and its flora, present a difficulty to the collector. Most of the fossils are on shales—and that crumbles to pieces so easily when it gets dry. To prevent this, dry it thoroughly, and put it in a shallow vessel (pie-plate) in which is some paraffin. Allow the whole arrangement to stand on a warm plate until the paraffin is melted, when the shale will soak it up, and, on cooling, be much more able to stand the risks of transportation.

A Caution.—Find out first from the specimen itself what the genus is—be it animal or plant. Then put on a provisional label, like this:

FAMILY.......................... No. ....
   GENUS.........................
   Specific name. ....
   Collected by.................... at ....
   Named by.....................

Don't stick the label on the fossil, but stick on a small bit of paper with a number on it to correspond with your label. If you have your labels printed, tell the printer to put them in nonpareil. We will suppose you have found a fossil; and on turning to the pictures in the Geology you find it looks like *Rynchonella capax*, or like *Spirifer Niagarensis*, or, it may be, *Orthis lynx*. You have here not only (3) genera, but (3) families represented. Now, which is it? Reference to Dana's handbook, page 170, tells you that the families are distinguished by differences of internal structure, that your specimen, being solid, gives no information about. Turn to Macfarlane's Geological

Railroad Guide, and you will find there the geology of the nearest station given. Discuss in your meeting why it should be an *Orthis* rather than a *Rynchonella*, and if still fairly puzzled send it to a specialist for name. Then destroy your provisional label, and put the same number on your final one. *Label nothing by guesswork.* Take nothing for granted, and don't send imperfect specimens, or too many kinds at once, for names to those willing to aid you.

In collecting rocks we should be careful to get clear, unweathered specimens, and, so far as practicable, carefully trim them to a uniform shape and size. For private or chapter collections, the specimens should be about $2\frac{1}{3} \times 3$ or 3×4 inches square, and one-half inch to one inch thick. The beginner will be surprised to find how much this careful selection and trimming of specimens adds to their appearance and value.

Specimens that are worth collecting are worth a little pains to keep them in good condition. Although minerals are hard, yet they are very easily injured or even ruined by rough handling, and especially by knocking or rubbing against one another. When starting on a collecting-trip, put a number of old newspapers in your bag, and then let each specimen be securely wrapped as soon as collected. Small wooden or pasteboard boxes are almost indispensable for fragile crystals and fossils. After each collecting-trip, your specimens should be carefully labeled, either by numbers referring to a catalogue, or by cards containing the name, locality, etc. The record of the locality is particularly important, since many kinds, especially of rocks, are rendered almost valueless by the loss of this interesting fact. Geological specimens will not bear huddling together; but their appearance is greatly enhanced by placing each by itself in a neat pasteboard tray, or on a block of wood ; and the label can then be attached to the beveled edge of the block.

As just explained, the ideal plan is for the student to collect his own specimens ; and it may be fairly said that for the *collector* specimens have an interest and value beyond what they would otherwise possess. It is, however, often impracticable to obtain suitable material in this way for a general course of study. The best plan then is, not to fall back on the books and dispense with the specimens, but to buy them. Those desiring to purchase minerals, rocks or fossils, will do well to send to Prof. W. O. Crosby, Boston Society of Natural History, Boston, Mass., for a catalogue of specimens and collections.

CHAPTER XI.

ARCHÆOLOGY AND ETHNOLOGY.

Perhaps we can help our students in this most interesting department in no better way than by presenting to them the following letter from our specialist, Mr. Hilborn T. Cresson, of Philadelphia:

From what I can learn upon the subject, many of our A. A. chapters have collections of ethnological and archæological specimens, such as bones from the shell-heaps and mounds, stone arrow-points from the graves of Tennessee, and surface 'finds,' stone axes, pipes, pottery, etc. It would certainly be a great source of satisfaction, if all the chapters of the A. A. throughout North and South America would unite in preserving archæological specimens, especially those of Tennessee, throughout the valley of the Mississippi, Florida—in fact, all our western and southern States. Specimens collected should be carefully labeled with precise details as to where found, whether in aboriginal mounds, cemeteries, graves, or surface of ground; by whom found and date of finding; occupation of person finding same, etc. (this last question indicates whether it be a professional dealer, picker, farmer, school-boy, or A. A. member; specimens obtained by the three last-named being much more reliable, we think, than those handled by the two former—especially if the object be of importance and rarity). Archæological specimens that are rough and uncouth in appearance and rudely made, should not be thrown aside for this reason. They are of great value, especially if from a mound or cemetery; nor should the smallest fragment of pottery be thrown aside. They all help to unravel the mystery about those beings who made them and have long since crumbled into dust. Photographs (*those made by members preferred*) of rare specimens in private collections are very valuable, if *minute details* in regard to them be preserved—very frequently upon the decease of their owner they are scattered to the four winds by the auctioneer's hammer, never to be reunited. They are in this case of little value for scientific study; the photographs, however, show them as they were before separation.

Specimens from one locality should be kept together. For example, if a shell-heap is examined (in exploration of a shell-heap, it *should be done in sections,* so that the *exact depth at which each object is found can be noted.* Samples should be taken at the *top, middle and bottom of the heap,* so as to show the actual condition of the material forming it ; and in order to study the fauna of the time the heap was being formed, large collections should be made of the different shells found in it, bones of fish, reptiles, birds and mammals), the articles collected from that particular heap should be kept together—not distributed at random throughout a cabinet. The object of this is obvious, from the fact that it shows the exact condition of the people who formed the heaps, the implements they used, the food they ate, and the animals that lived at that period. Specimens from mounds and graves should be treated in a like manner. Members should never explore mounds, graves, or cemeteries of aboriginal man unless they be conducted by, or under the direction of, an Agassiz Association specialist, or other professional archæologist, who may direct the operation in a proper manner. Much harm has been done in this way by ignorant persons. *Never open a mound by the old method of digging a hole in the centre.* The earth should be removed section by section. We will furnish details to chapters that may desire them in cases where immediate action is necessary, as in exploring a mound that has to be removed or leveled. Photographs of mounds, earthworks, and cemeteries, with careful drawings, surveys, measurements, and maps (of their exact position) are of great value. If the mounds have been excavated, details should be obtained as to methods pursued by the excavators in opening them, the articles found therein, and what became of them. If the possessors thereof will not present them to the Association, to be forwarded to some museum and preserved for the interests of science, photographs should be taken, and endeavors made to induce wealthy citizens to purchase and present them to some museum in good standing. The Peabody Museum of Archæology and Ethnology at Cambridge, Massachusetts, Frederick Ward Putnam, Esq., Professor and Curator, is probably the best conducted museum of this kind in America. If the Indian grave, burial-mound, or cemetery remain intact, the owners of the property on which it has been discovered ought to be applied to at once for the sole right to excavate it in the interests of science. This will prevent the wanton destruction of Indian mounds by dealers in (so-called) Indian relics. We earnestly appeal to all the Agassiz Association chapters to defeat, if possible, the desecration of Indian mounds, cemeteries, and graves by the vandals referred to. Let our chapters get up entertainments and form a fund for their purchase and presentation. Old and young should respond cheerfully to this suggestion. In this way aboriginal monuments that are fast disappearing before the onward march of civilization can be preserved, at least until a scientific examination can be made of their contents.

Some day, I hope, the Agassiz Association Museum will be formed, and among its various departments may that of ethnology and archæology be pushed with vigor. If I am not misinformed you have already dreamed of this. Assuredly some well-filled pockets will aid the great work that you are directing.

More especially since the publication of *The Swiss Cross* do inquiries reach me from the Western States and South America. Many of these are from persons who seem deeply interested in early man, and his descendants who occupy our reservations, still wander over certain districts of the far north, or dwell in the forests of South America. Quite frequently I have packages forwarded to me from elderly persons for classification and examination. In many cases the specimens are supposed to have been found under circumstances that verge on the marvelous. These are generally purchases from unreliable dealers in antiquities, and are not 'finds' made by themselves; hence they are apt to prove counterfeits, which at the present time are made in large quantities throughout the Western and Middle States. I deem it necessary to warn all our chapters against notorious gangs of counterfeiters (of mound specimens) that exist in Ohio, others in Illinois and Kentucky, and last, but not least, against those clumsy 'antiques' that emanate from the *marble yards of Philadelphia.*

CHAPTER XII.

No question has been more frequently repeated than "What can be done in the Winter?"

First of all may be mentioned the study of minerals. What can be more delightful than to analyze with blowpipe and test-tube the specimens gathered from cliff and quarry during the open months. Directions for this work are to be found in any of the manuals referred to in the list of books, which is given on another page.

Chemistry is another science which can be pursued in winter as well as summer, and as it lies at the base of nearly all the other natural sciences, students in other departments may well devote the time when they are debarred by weather from outdoor work to its cultivation. In fact, however, there is hardly a branch of natural history that cannot be followed even out-of-doors for many days of every month in the year.

One of the things which those who live in cities can do, is to make drawings of snow-crystals, to exchange for specimens more easily found in the country. Catch the crystals, as they fall, on a dark cloth. Look at them through a magnifying-glass, if you have one, and draw as well as you can from memory. Photograph them if possible.

The drawings should be made of a uniform diameter of half an inch. Six drawings may be made nicely on a card as large as a postal-card. For convenience in exchanging, we all may make them of the same size and arrange them in the same way, as follows :

SNOW CRYSTALS.   DRAWN BY CORWIN LINSON.

To have these crystal pictures valuable, we must notice the conditions which prevail as the snow falls. Look at the thermometer and barometer, and note the strength of the wind, as well as the date. Attention to these details will enable us to decide whether or not snow-crystals vary in shape with heat and cold and density of air, etc.

The frost-pictures on the window, too, are well worthy your attention. Each form is fashioned according to some fixed law ; yet so varied are the beautiful shapes, so intricate the crystalline curves and angles, that it requires much patient study to trace the operation of cause and effect. Many of our members have photographic outfits, and they could render valuable service by securing pictures of these fairy frost-pencillings.

Indoors, again, the microscope reveals a world rivalling in beauty and infinity of extent the outer world that is open to our unaided vision ; and this instrument can be used in the city as well as in the country, and in winter as well as in summer.

Another thing you of the city can do, is to suspend seeds in bottles over water, and study the growth of different plants as the tiny leaves unroll. Make neat cases also for insects or minerals, and exchange them for specimens. Collect specimens of veneers from cabinet and piano shops, and prepare them for exchange. Nearly all the grains, and nuts, and spices, and fabrics, and seeds, and barks, and woods, and metals, can be found in city shops, and for these you can readily get anything you may wish from the country. Again, many of you have books or pictures on subjects of natural history which are old to you, but which some member of the Association would be very thankful to get. These also can be exchanged.

Besides these things, we need only mention birds' nests abandoned in leafless trees, cocoons suspended from bushes and tucked away under fence-rails, beetles burrowing in old stumps, sections of wood and bark, cones and buds, to show that there is plenty of outdoor work, even in winter; while, indoors, cabinets are to be built, specimens determined, labeled, and arranged, philosophical experiments performed, books read, letters written, exchanges made.

Many of our members capture caterpillars and other insects in the fall, and keep them during the winter, watching their curious habits and wonderful transformations, as is detailed in the following bright letter :

DEAR MR. BALLARD,—I have been reading "Insect Lives." It is the nicest book I have ever read.* I could read a whole library full of books just like that. I am getting on famously

---

* INSECT LIVES, by MRS. JULIA P. BALLARD, is published at one dollar by the WRITERS PUBLISHING COMPANY, 21 University Place, New York, N. Y. We know of no better book for the beginner in the study of butterflies and moths.

with my collection. But one of my caterpillars does act so funny. It is the caterpillar of that moth — the *Polyphemus*, is it? I found him two days ago, and put him in my box. He seemed very sluggish. If I turned him over, he would very slowly turn himself over back again ; but I thought perhaps he was going to change his skin, or something like that. The next afternoon I looked at him, and there were hundreds of little worms coming out of holes in his skin (horrid things!). I was going to burn him up, but decided to wait and see what would come of it. The next morning nearly all of them had changed into little grayish-brown cocoons, and tumbled off, leaving tiny holes in his skin, and now he is twisting about like a good fellow.

ANNIE BOSWORTH.

The sequel to this tragedy was told in a subsequeut letter from the same writer.

"My poor worm died the day after I wrote you, and a day or two after the little rice-houses began to open, and hundreds of tiny flies came out from them, but I threw them away in disgust."

CHAPTER XIII.

ONE of the pleasantest features of the A. A. is the exchange of specimens between members. Some hints may be helpful. When you have duplicates which you wish to exchange, decide as nearly as possible what you wish in return. Send your request, tersely written to the President. It will appear in *The Swiss Cross* in either one or two months. The magazine is printed some time before it is issued, so that you should send any notice at least a month before you wish to see it in print. In preparing packages for the mail, be sure that you enclose the specimens in a box sufficiently strong to withstand the frequent concussions of the way, and so securely wrapped and tied that it shall not become undone. About one-third of the packages received here are broken on the way. Minerals should be separately wrapped in paper or cloth before being put into the box. Eggs may safely be sent in auger-holes bored in little blocks of wood. Flowers and ferns should be carefully inclosed between strong sides of pasteboard. Insects should be pinned with the utmost possible strength and care into boxes thoroughly lined with cork, very strong, light, and doubly wrapped. Beetles and bugs may be sent in cotton, like eggs. Always prepay postage in full. Inclose no writing in the package (except the labels of the specimens, which are allowed), but never neglect to accompany the package with a postal-card or letter, describing contents, stating from whom it comes, and rehearsing what you expect to receive in exchange. It is often utterly impossible to determine the sender of a package, or to know what to send in return. Tie the parcel strongly, but do not seal it, unless you wish to pay letter postage. One or two fine specimens are always more acceptable than several inferior ones. No propositions for exchange can be noticed in *The Swiss Cross*, excepting from subscribers, or from members of the A. A. For this, among other reasons, it is necessary for us to keep a full register of all members, and names of new members should always be sent us at once.

Whenever any one writes proposing an exchange, courtesy requires him to enclose a stamp for reply. Requests of this nature should always be promptly answered. Aim to give rather more than you receive. A grasping spirit of trade is utterly foreign to the nature of a true scientist.

CHAPTER XIV.

REPORTS FROM CHAPTERS AND CORRESPONDING MEMBERS.

PERHAPS the actual working of our Society cannot better be illustrated than by giving a few extracts from the thousands of letters that constantly come to us from our friends of the A. A. We shall select such as contain practical suggestions for work ; and the first shows what may be done in the way of out-door excursions :

SALT LAKE CITY, Utah.

I write to inform you of the organization of a Chapter of the Agassiz Association in Salt Lake City. Several of us boys have been more or less interested in natural history for some time, and when we read about the A. A., we thought that it was just what we wanted. So on Wednesday, August 2nd, four of us met and organized the chapter.

We have already taken several tramps after specimens. On the first one we found the terminal moraine of a glacier, and our honorary member gave us a long description of glaciers—the manner of their formation and movements, and the way in which moraines are formed. Our last trip was to a mining district situated 9,300 feet above the sea. It lasted five days, and we walked sixty miles, and found many rare Alpine plants, fossils, minerals, and bugs.

FRED. E. LEONARD.

The next shows how Boards of Education help us :

HYDE PARK, Illinois.

I am happy to inform you that a Natural History Association has been formed in our High School. We have seventeen members, all of whom are enthusiastic in their work. We all desire to connect ourselves with the A. A. We had a cabinet made, which cost $25.00. The Board of Education has kindly advanced the cost of this, provided we leave our collection in the building. They also allow us to meet in the building. We have an entrance fee of 50 cents, in order that none but workers may join. We are very careful about electing new members.

W. R. GWYNN.

Among our most delightful branches are what we call 'Family Chapters,' in which the members of one family unite to form a little society and study together.

FLUSHING, L. I.

I want to tell you how much we enjoy our meetings. The subject of the last meeting was Mistletoe, and here is what was said about it. Mamma said, "The botanical name of the mistletoe is *Viscum album.* In olden times it was thought to be poisonous, for Shakespeare speaks of the 'baleful mistletoe.' The Druids used it in religious rites. It is a parasite, growing chiefly on apple-trees." Miss Scott had tasted the berry, which is sweet and glutinous. She painted me a lovely picture of mistletoe and holly. In the evenings when papa is at home, we have music, and, if possible, pieces bearing on our subject ; for instance, this evening we had a song entitled 'The Mistletoe Bough,' and an instrumental piece, the 'Mistletoe Polka.' Mamma plays on the violin, and I on the organ or piano.

From your friend, F. M. H.

There is no limit with regard to age. Little children have bright eyes.

THE OAKS, TIOGA CENTER, N. Y.

I am nine, and my sister is five. We have examined a geranium-bug, and it is beautiful. Its body is green, and it has six legs that are clear like crystal. The antennæ are longer than the insect, and are sometimes thrown backward. It has a long beak. The body has two horns at the end. The eyes are reddish brown, with tiny white dots.

ANGIE LATIMER, Sec.

Several of our chapters publish local papers.

MACOMB, Ill.

Progressing nicely. We meet at each other's houses every Friday afternoon after school. Almost all of us have been collecting insects during the summer. We have a paper read every two weeks, to which we contribute original articles on anything pertaining to natural history. The chapter is divided into two parts, and each part edits the paper alternately. We cannot understand how other chapters have so nice club-rooms and cabinets and microscopes, etc. Where do they get their money? We like the A. A. *very much.*

NELLIE H. TUNNICLIFF.

The next letter shows how to raise money when it is needed.

BUFFALO, N. Y.

Our report is somewhat tardy, owing to an entertainment given for our microscope fund. We realized $35, which, with the amount on hand, gives us about $100 to invest in a good instrument. Our chapter has increased to twenty-four active and two honorary members. Owing to the lateness of the season, we have collectively made but one excursion, though individually we have not been idle.

CORA FREEMAN.

The girls are as enthusiastic workers as the boys.

We are pupils of the Waco Female College, Texas. About four years ago our teacher began to teach us to love nature, and, to keep our eyes and ears open, often took us to the woods. Oh, how we enjoyed those rambles! Such rides to and from the woods! We soon got a collection, and determined to form a Natural History Society. We were deliberating on a name when, to our great joy, your first article was read to us. We forthwith adopted the name, constitution, and by-laws. Since then we have varied with wind and weather, but have now launched upon a smooth-sailing sea. We have twenty-six members. Some of our prominent citizens have joined us. By carefully hoarding our dues of admission, etc., we have been able to buy a fine microscope, a number of shells, and a few books and pictures. We have a book in which the librarian pastes articles and pictures selected by some one member every week. We have another into which the secretary transcribes the papers read by the members before the society, and also articles of interest which cannot be cut from valuable books. The president always appoints one member to ask three questions to be answered at the next meeting. The correct answers are copied into our manuscript scrap-book. Oh, we have so much to say to you, and to ask, I hardly know where to begin or leave off! We have a specimen of the Texas centipede for exchange, also a stinging lizard and a horned frog.　　　　JENNY WISE.

LEDYARD, Conn.

We live far apart from one another, and on cold winter evenings it is quite an effort to drive two or three miles to a meeting; but we have held them just the same, with hardly an exception. We bought a mineral collection, and studied the specimens in order, bringing our own specimens to compare with them. Memorial Day we celebrated by an excursion to Lantern Hill. Twenty-two of us reached the foot of the hill before noon, and there had singing and select readings from *The Swiss Cross*. After dinner we climbed the hill. Orchids, star-flowers, and ragwort excited remark among our botanists. We chiselled 'A. A. '87' upon the bark of a chestnut oak, gave three cheers for Agassiz and three for our chapter, and then wended our way to the silex-works. Here each member tried to find a large crystal, several succeeding in getting them as large as a man's thumb. Besides these we brought home handfuls of the powdered silex, which is sent to New York to be made into crockery, paint—*and sugar*. In the fall we hope to purchase books, and raise money for a course of scientific lectures. "So, high in hope, we wait the summer through."　　　　MARY A. AVERY.

And our ranks are recruited by an increasing number of adult members, who are equally welcome.

NEW BRUNSWICK, N. J., Oct., 1887.

MY DEAR SIR,—We are now under full steam; eighty-eight members; list increasing rapidly. We have organized sections under which the members register *a la* the American Association for the Advancement of Science, as follows: Microscopy, Dr. A. V. N. Baldwin; Botany, Dr. N. Williamson; Photography, P. T. Austen, Ph.D.; Zoology, Professor Van Dyck; Astronomy, Professor Merriman; Natural Philosophy, Mr. Ranney; Geology, Professor Cook; Meteorology, Professor McGann; Ornithology, Dr. C. H. Voorhees. Membership will probably strike about 200.

Yours, very truly,

PETER T. AUSTEN.

When a wide-awake teacher takes hold of the matter, the most important results follow.

About six months ago, Chapter 266 A. A. was organized in connection with my school. We have succeeded wonderfully, both in point of numbers and collections. We now number thirty-three, and the prospects are that we shall soon have as many more. The boys, some twenty or more, have over five hundred specimens, consisting of fossils and insects. The girls, of whom we have lately added a dozen, are busily engaged in gathering leaves, roots, and seeds, and, when they make a report, we shall classify them botanically. The whole neighborhood has been awakened by the enthusiasm of the boys and girls. All this work is collateral ; that is, no part of school-time is taken up. The County Superintendent of Schools was so delighted with the idea, that he has earnestly requested me to bring the matter before our County Institute, the third week in December. The Institute numbers six hundred teachers, and if this is done, the A. A., no doubt, will spread in this county.

T. G. Jones, St. Clair, Schuyl. Co., Pa.

Another marked instance is that of Chapter 285, Greenfield, Mass., as shown by this extract from the *Springfield Republican :*

"Principal Sanderson started a good deal of zeal among the high-school pupils, some two years ago, in the study of natural history, and as a result the natural history society was organized. The work began in a small way in the collection of birds, plants, and minerals, until the foundation has been laid for a permanent museum. The society now has one large case of stuffed birds, containing 150 well preserved specimens. These are mostly native birds, caught and mounted by members of the society. Several in this way have become quite expert taxidermists. The society belongs to the Agassiz Association, and by exchanges has added to some of the departments. The local organization is made up of thirty-six members, who were ambitious enough, last fall, to hire of the town the old brick house near the high-school building, paying a rental of $150 a year. These youthful scientific investigators want encouragement from the citizens at large, and are going to ask the town, at its annual meeting, to contribute the rent of this building. It would seem that the voters could very properly encourage the young people in this way. As the natural history rooms are located close to the high-school building, it can very readily be made a beneficial adjunct to the public schools. Already the zoological classes have enjoyed the advantages of these rooms and their collections."

Mr. Sanderson is no longer living, but 'The Sanderson Chapter,' named in his honor, is still growing and prospering.

Young men can accomplish excellent results by themselves.

NEW YORK, N. Y.

In looking over the records of the year, I was pleased to find that it has been a very prosperous and successful year for our chapter. Standing forward in bold relief, we find several facts, among which may be mentioned our evening entertainment, which, thanks to the generous help of our friends, brought us a clear profit of over one hundred dollars. Then there is the enormous increase in membership, which was greatly due to the circular issued by the executive committee, wherein they called attention to the work carried on by the chapter, and requested gentlemen who might not be able to take active part in the work of the chapter, to join us nevertheless, and thereby encourage the growth of it. The number of members on roll in December, 1885, was thirty-one ; in December, 1886, it was sixty, an increase of twenty-nine. It is pleasing to note, that, although many strange faces have joined us, still the sociability and good feeling which always prevailed among us have not abated, but increased. Then there was the celebration of our fifth anniversary, and at the same time that of Agassiz's birthday. Mr. A. W. Miller sent us an invitation to meet at his house, our old headquarters, which we thankfully accepted. The members enjoyed a very pleasant evening ; many speeches were made and toasts offered. We have had during this year nineteen lectures and discussions, all of which were of an instructive and interesting nature. A number of evenings have been profitably spent under ' Notes and News,' where we exchanged our knowledge of interesting things, which were too short to make up a lecture. The members can undoubtedly recall the pleasant times they have had this summer at the chapter excursions to Mamaroneck ; the two-days' excursion to Morristown, and, on invitation from the Torrey Club, to Annandale, Staten Island ; the moth-hunts to East New York, which, I am sorry to say, are the last, because the woods have been sold, and the privileges we there enjoyed are at an end. Then the excursions of the Curator's Committee, to which all members were welcome, to Tarrytown Heights, Staten Island, Perth Amboy, and other places, were very pleasant. Quite an improvement has been made by the Curator's Committee on our old way of choosing subjects for lectures, by preparing a calendar for each month, which is sent to all the members, thus also giving the lecturer more time to prepare. The Curator's Committee have also made Tuesday evenings an interesting feature. These evenings are spent in preparing specimens for the cabinet, and usually one of the curators gives a short lecture.

One Tuesday evening of each month is set aside for what they call 'exhibition night,' when they show and explain the specimens to the friends of members. The cabinet is apparently in excellent condition : it contains about twenty-two hundred different kinds of specimens, also many miscellaneous curiosities and many instruments. We have received during the year numerous kind donations, of which I make mention of one hundred specimens from the disbanded Fairview Chapter, and nineteen specimens of marble from Mr. Rückert. A good variety of books may now be found in our library : there are 315 volumes and many hundred magazines and pamphlets.

SECRETARY OF CHAPTER 87.

JAMAICA PLAIN, Mass.

The past year has been very encouraging to us. It began rather unfavorably. We were obliged to leave the small house in which we had met. We soon found new quarters in the unoccupied harness-room of a barn ; but we had no means of heating it, and when cold weather set in we returned to our old method of meeting at members' houses. But we needed a place we could be sure of, and at last decided to have a small house built. We got up a stock company called the 'Agassiz Building Company,' and issued one hundred shares of the par value of one dollar. These were quickly taken by our friends, and a house 12 x 18 feet was built on land belonging to the father of one of our members. It is painted yellow, with olive trimmings, and the roof is red. We pay rent to the treasurer of the company, and out of this, at the end of the year, five per cent. is paid on the stock, and the remainder is spent in redeeming the shares, so that finally we shall own the house. We have a flagstaff and a flag. The flag has a red cross on a yellow ground, with ' 760 ' in white on the cross and a red 'A' on each side of the upper arm, and is kept flying when we have our meetings. Several of the meetings of the Boston Assembly have been held at the Chapter House. We have quite a collection of minerals, and are adding to it all the time. We built a piazza in front of our house ourselves. We opened it with a reception, June 4, to which about seventy of our friends came—not all at once, but between 4.30 and 8.30 We have just had a stove put in, and are preparing for cold weather. Wishing the A. A. success,

C. S. GREENE.

Chapters in which both sexes, young and old, teachers and pupils, unite, have been equally successful. Witness the following report from our largest chapter, which has grown up under the affectionate care of Professor E. Adams Hartwell :

FITCHBURG, Mass.

We organized, as you know, in January, 1886, our present chapter being formed by the union of four smaller chapters previously existing here, and on February 5 held our first regular meeting. With one exception, meetings have been held once in two weeks since then. Fourteen members were registered at our organization, and since that time our growth has been steady. We have registered on our books up to date one hundred and forty-two names. At first our meetings were held in a room in the high-school building ; but, as our membership increased, we felt the need of more convenient quarters, and accordingly in September we hired a hall on Main Street, where we have our cabinets and hold our meetings. We have had built two cabinets 4′ x 7′ x 12″, to hold our large collections of minerals, shells, birds, bottled specimens, etc. We have also a valuable herbarium of over five hundred specimens. In addition to these we have a few magazines and pamphlets, and hope some day to own a good library. On May 28 we celebrated with appropriate exercises and great success the birthday of Agassiz. On that occasion we had on exhibition our collections, both individual and collective. At our meetings members are encouraged to bring in reports of observations, items of scientific interest found in papers and magazines, specimens of various kinds, etc. The principal exercises of the evening consist of essays or debates, varied occasionally by the introduction of a mock trial or a mock senate. Last autumn a committee was appointed to investigate the mineral wealth of Rollstone, where the granite-quarries are, and they presented not long since a very interesting report of their researches. In the spring we shall expect a similar report from a committee appointed to investigate Pearl Hill, another of our landmarks. During the spring and summer, in addition to our bi-weekly meeting, we had several field excursions, when we took long walks into the country. Early in July a picnic was held at a lake a few miles from here. While the greater part of our members are young people from the schools, mostly the high-school, however, we have several teachers and some of the city's merchants in our ranks.

NELLIE F. MARSHALL, *Secretary.*

Valuable libraries and reading-rooms are founded in connection with the A. A.

MONTREAL, Canada.

We have a splendid cabinet, six feet high, three feet wide, and two feet deep, containing forty-eight drawers, twenty-two of which are allotted to the entomological section. Nineteen of these are already filled with insects. Our library promises to become a great success. We are trying to secure a room in the St. Antoine School for a museum and reading-room. We have had two very successful field-meetings, on one of which prizes were offered for the best collection made during the day. I expect to see the Montreal branch of the A. A. take a leading position among the scientific institutions of Canada. One of our most successful evenings was spent with the microscope.

W. D. SHAW.

Mr. Shaw, who was one of the brightest and most promising young men in the Association, died about a year ago, at the early age of nineteen, leaving a name beloved and honored wherever it was known.

GREENUP, Ky., December, 1887.

The Public Library formed here under our auspices has now a thousand volumes, and we are busy cataloguing them.

Mrs. GEORGE GIBBS.

In some cases members take turns in giving lectures.

We have given a parlor concert. C. K. Linson gave us a 'chalk talk.' At one side of the parlor we had a table with some specimens on it, and after the entertainment we invited our friends to inspect them. We have now money enough to get a cabinet. We have decided to have a course of lectures—one delivered by each member on his chosen branch.

A. D. PHILLIPS, Brooklyn, E. D.

A love for Nature often affects the whole character.

But the best of all, and that for which I want sincerely to thank the A. A. and its projector, is the result of the work in one particular case. As a teacher, you know how difficult it is to do just the best- thing with a roguish, careless boy, smart, but caring little for study and with little or no will to work. Geology last year and chemistry this prepared him for an elementary course in determinative mineralogy. This he has undertaken, under the guise of association work, and to this we largely attribute a most wonderful improvement in the boy. Spare moments are spent in the laboratory instead of in mischief ; he has begged to return to Latin, which he had dropped, and bids fair to stand at or near the head of his class in that and other studies. Instead of lawless lounging at recess, he is quiet and gentlemanly.

A FRIEND.

CHAPTER XV.

BOOKS RECOMMENDED.

(The figures refer to the Publishers' addresses given below. Books marked * are illustrated.)

DIVISION I.

ASTRONOMY.	Price.	Pub's No.
G. B. Airy. *Popular Astronomy.	$1 10	48
R. S. Ball. *Elements of Astronomy.	2 25	29
C. Flammarion *The Atmosphere.	2 00	36
*Astronomical Myths.	5 00	36
A. Guillemin. *The Heavens.	4 50	47
*The Sun.	1 50	47
*Wonders of the Moon.	1 50	47
*The World of Comets.	7 00	47
J. F. W. Herschell. *Outlines of Astronomy.	4 00	29
D. Kirkwood. Meteoric Astronomy.	1 50	61
*Comets and Meteors.	1 25	61
J. K. Lockyer. *Elements of Astronomy.	1 25	29
*Studies in Spectrum Analysis.	2 50	29
O. M. Mitchel. Planetary and Stellar Worlds.	—	28
E. Neison. *The Moon and the Configurations of its Surface.	10 00	40
S. Newcomb and E. S. Holden. *Astronomy for High Schools.	2 50	38
Briefer course.	1 25	38
J. A. Westwood Oliver. *Astronomy for Amateurs.	2 25	40
R. A. Proctor. *The Orbs Around Us.	1 75	40
*Other Worlds than Ours.	1 75	29
*The Moon.	2 00	29
*The Universe of Stars	3 50	40
*Star Atlas (large).	6 00	40
*Star Atlas (new).	1 75	40
*The Poetry of Astronomy.	2 25	40
*The Stars in their Seasons.	2 00	40
*Myths and Marvels of Astronomy.	2 25	40
G. W. Plympton. *The Star Finder.	1 00	48
H. E. Roscoe. *Spectrum Analysis.	6 00	42

ASTRONOMY—*Cont'd.*	Price.	*Pub's No.*
H. Schellen. *Spectrum Analysis. Ed. by Huggins. With maps	$6 00	29
T. W. Webb. Celestial Objects for Common Telescopes.	3 00	40

BIOLOGY AND EVOLUTION.

	Price.	Pub's No.
Grant Allen. *Flowers and their Pedigrees.	1 50	29
F. Jeffrey Bell. *Elements of Comparative Anatomy.	—	—
Edward Clodd. *The Story of Creation. A plain story of Evolution.	1 75	40
Charles Darwin. Origin of Species.	2 00	29
Descent of Man.	3 00	29
*Movements and Habits of Climbing Plants.	1 25	29
*Fertilization of Orchids by Insects.	1 75	29
Cross and Self-Fertilization in the Vegetable Kingdom.	2 00	29
*Different Forms of Flowers on Plants of the Same Species.	1 50	29
*The Power of Movement in Plants.	2 00	29
Insectivorous Plants.	2 00	29
Vegetable Mould and Earthworms.	1 50	29
Variations of Animals and Plants.	5 00	29
R. J. Harvey Gibson. Elementary Biology.	1 75	40
G. B. Howes. An Atlas of Practical Elementary Biology.	4 00	42
E. Haeckel. *The Evolution of Man. 2 vols.	5 00	29
*The History of Creation. 2 vols.	5 00	29
T. H. Huxley and H. N. Martin. A Course of Elementary Instruction in Practical Biology.	2 60	42
T. H. Huxley. Origin of Species.	1 00	29
Lectures on Evolution.	15	34
Physical Basis of Life.	15	34
A Manual of the Anatomy of Invertebrate Animals.	2 50	29
A Manual of the Anatomy of Vertebrate Animals.	2 50	29
*Man's Place in Nature.	1 25	29
Charles Letourneau. Biology. Translated by W. Maccall.	1 50	61
J. Lubbock. *British Wild Flowers in Relation to Insects.	1 25	42
T. C. Magginly. *Biology.	1 25	34

	Price.	Pub's No.
BIOLOGY AND EVOLUTION—*Cont'd.*		
H. N. Martin and W. A. Moale. *Hand-book of Vertebrate Dissection. 3 parts. Each.	$0 60	42
H. A. Nicholson. *Introduction to the Study of Biology.	60	29
William Noble. *Hours with a Three-Inch Telescope.	1 50	40
T. Jeffrey Parker. A Course of Instruction in Zoötomy.	2 25	42
Geo. J. Romanes. Animal Intelligence.	1 75	29
Wm. Sedgwick and E. B. Wilson. General Biology.	—	38
Karl Semper. Animal Life as Affected by the Natural Conditions of Existence.	2 00	29
S. H. Stevenson *Boys and Girls in Biology.	1 50	29
John Tyndall. *Floating Matter in the Air, in Relation to Putrefaction.	1 50	29
Robert Wiedersheim. Elements of the Comparative Anatomy of Vertebrates. Translated by W. N. Parker.	3 00	42
J. H. Wythe. Easy Lessons in Vegetable Biology.	40	43

CHEMISTRY.

	Price.	Pub's No.
A. H. Allen. Commercial Organic Analysis. 3 vols.	—	71
H. E. Armstrong. Introduction to the Study of Organic Chemistry.	1 50	29
D. Allfield. Medical Chemistry.	2 00	60
—— Barker. College Chemistry.	1 50	10
C. L. Bloxam. *Laboratory Teaching.	1 75	59
F. W. Clarke. The Elements of Chemistry. 1884.	1 40	29
J. P. Cooke, Jr. The New Chemistry.	2 00	29
W. Crookes. *Select Methods of Chemical Analysis.	8 00	40
Douglas and Prescott. *Qualitative Analysis. 1881.	3 50	48
G. E. R. Ellis. *Introduction to Practical Organic Analysis.	50	40
G. Fownes. *Manual. 2 vols.	7 00	59
Frankland and Japp. Inorganic Chemistry.	—	71
C. R. Fresenius. *Qualitative Analysis.	4 00	50
*Quantitative Analysis.	7 00	50
W. Jago. *Inorganic Chemistry.	75	40
Kolbe's *Short Text-book of Inorganic Chemistry.	2 50	40

CHEMISTRY—*Cont'd.*	Price.	Pub's No.
Lewis. Chemical Labels.	$0 50	48
Carl Lange. *Sulphuric Acid and Alkali. 1879.	12 50	75
Jean Macé. The History of a Mouthful of Bread. Translated by Mrs. Gatty.	1 75	36
Wm. Allen Miller. Introduction to Inorganic Chemistry.	1 50	29
Clifford Mitchell, M.D. Dental Chemistry.	1 25	9
Campbell Morfitt. *Mineral Phosphates. 1873.	20 00	74
C. Plattner. *Blowpipe Analysis. (Translated.) 1885.	5 00	48
*Payen's Industrial Chemistry.	10 50	40
A. B. Prescott. *Proximate Organic Analysis. 1887.	5 00	48
G. W. Rains. *Exercises in Qualitative Analysis.	50	29
Ira Remsen. Introduction to the Study of Chemistry.	1 40	38
J. Emerson Reynolds. Experimental Chemistry.	1 20	40
Roscoe and Schorlemmer. Treatise on Chemistry. 6 vols.	24 00	29
V. von Richter. *Organic Chemistry. Translated by Smith.	3 00	59
F. H. Storer, S. B. Agriculture in some of its Relations with Chemistry. 2 vols.	5 00	47
A. Strecker. *Text-book of Organic Chemistry.	5 00	29
F. Sutton. Volumetric Analysis.	5 00	59
T. E. Thorpe. *Quantitative Chemical Analysis.	1 50	40
Thorpe and Muir. *Qualitative Analysis and Laboratory Practice.	1 50	29
William A. Tilden. Introduction to the Study of Chemical Philosophy.	1 50	29
Practical Chemistry.	45	40
H. W. Tyler. Entertainment in Chemistry.	55	7
H. Watts. Dictionary of Chemistry. An Encyclopædia. 9 vols.	75 00	40
R. Wagner. *Chemical Technology.	5 00	29
Ad. Wurtz. The Atomic Theory.	1 50	29
Wanklyn and Chapman. Water Analysis. 1876.	75	74

[N.B.—The best general book on Chemistry is Fownes's Manual. Wagner gives an excellent description of chemical processes as applied to technical arts. For the laboratory, Fresenius's books are the standard guides, but the works of Douglas and of Prescott are also good, and more recent. For a beginner, Cooke's 'New Chemistry,' and Barker's 'College Chemistry,' are excellent. The latter has descriptive chemistry last, and hence the last part should be read first by the tyro. The first part is a concise and accurate synopsis of chemical theory as now understood, and the student should read it carefully as he is able to understand it.]

GEOLOGY AND PETROGRAPHY.	Price.	Pub's No.
Louis Agassiz. Geological Sketches. 2 vols., ea.	$1 50	19
E. B. Andrews. Elementary Geology of the Interior States. 432 illustrations.	1 17	55
C. R. Boyd, M.E. *Resources of Southwest Virginia.	3 00	50
Bernhard von Cotta. Rocks Classified and Described.	5 00	40
James Croll. *Climate and Time.	2 50	29
W. O. Crosby. Common Minerals and Rocks. 40c. ; cloth, 60c. Fifty labeled specimens.	2 00	16
J. D. Dana. Geological Story Briefly Told.	1 35	39
Text-book of Geology.	2 30	39
Manual of Geology.	4 45	39
J. W. Dawson. Acadian Geology.	6 50	42
Story of the Earth and Man.	—	—
*The Geological History of Plants.	1 75	29
Archibald Geikie. Physical Geography (*Science Primer*).	45	29
Class-book of Physical Geography.	1 10	42
Geology (*Science Primer.*)	45	29
Class-book of Geology.	2 60	42
Text-book of Geology.	7 50	42
Outlines of Field Geology.	1 00	42
J. Geikie. Great Ice Age.	2 50	29
Gilbert. Lake Bonneville.	—	3
H. C. Hovey. Celebrated American Caverns.	2 00	54
E. Hull. Building and Ornamental Stones.	3 50	42
T. S. Hunt. Mineral Physiology and Physiography.	5 00	15
Alpheus Hyatt. Pebbles.	15	18
J. W. Judd. *Volcanoes.	2 00	29
Charles Kingsley. Town Geology.	15	34
Joseph Le Conte. Compend of Geology.	1 40	29
Elements of Geology.	4 00	29

GEOLOGY AND PETROGRAPHY—*Cont'd.*	*Price.*	*Pub's No.*
J. Macfarlane. *Coal Regions of America.	$5 00	29
*American Geological Railway Guide.	1 50	29
G. A. Mantell. Petrifactions and their Teachings	2 50	61
H. A. Nicholson. Manual of Paleontology.	76	29
Life History of the Earth.	2 00	29
*Text-book of Geology.	1 25	29
John Phillips. Manual of Geology.	—	79
R. Pumpelly. *Geology. (Text-book.)	2 50	38
Joseph Prestwich. Text-book of Geology. 2 vols.	15 25	42
E. Reclus. *The Earth.	5 00	36
*The Ocean.	6 00	36
W. B. Rogers. Geology of the Virginias.	5 00	29
Russell. History of Lake Lahontan.	1 50	3
Frank Rutley. The Study of Rocks.	1 75	29
N. S. Shaler. First Book in Geology.	1 00	18
T. D. Steele. New Popular Geology	1 25	30
John Tyndall. Forms of Water.	1 50	29
*Glaciers of the Alps. (Scarce.)	—	—
A. R. Wallace. Island Life.	4 00	36
S. G. Williams. *Applied Geology.	1 40	29
Alexander Winchell. *World Life.	2 50	6
Sparks from a Geologist's Hammer.	2 00	6
*Sketches of Creation.	2 00	36
Geological Excursions for Young Learners	1 50	6

United States Geological Survey : Annual Reports,
Monographs, Bulletins. To be obtained
at cost on application to the Director U. S.
Geological Survey, Washington, D. C.

Reports on the Geology of Canada. Application
should be made to the Director Geological
Survey, Ottawa, Canada.

Reports on the Geology of various States, especially New Hampshire, New York, New
Jersey, Pennsylvania, Ohio, Michigan, Indiana, Illinois, Wisconsin, Minnesota,
Iowa, Missouri and California. Uusually
to be obtained through the State Geologist,
State Librarian, or Members of the Legis-
lature.

American Journal of Science, New Haven. Per year.	6 00	
American Geologist, Minneapolis.	3 00	
Geological Magazine, London.	—	

PALEONTOLOGY.

	Price.	Pub's No.
L. Lesquereux. Coal Flora of Pennsylvania. 3 vols. With atlas. Pennsylvania Geological Survey.	—	—
G. A. Mantell. Petrifactions and their Teachings	$2 00	29
H. A. Nicholson. Ancient Life History of the Earth.	2 00	29
Paleontology.	5 00	79
S. H. Scudder. Fossil Butterflies of North America.	—	26
L. Ward. Sketch of Paleo-botany. Fifth Annual Report of U. S. Geological Survey.	—	—

PHYSICS.

	Price.	Pub's No.
N. Arnott. *Elements of Physics.	3 00	29
*Park Benjamin.	2 00	47
L. Blodgett. *Climatology of United States.	5 00	61
A. Daniell. *Text-book of Physics.	3 50	42
A. Ganot. *Physics.	5 00	51
E. A. Dolbear. *The Art of Projecting. New edition.	2 00	20
R. F. Glazebrook. *Physical Optics.	2 25	29
R. F. Glazebrook and Shaw. *Practical Physics.	2 25	29
W. R. Grove. *The Correlation of Physical Forces.	2 00	29
T. H. Huxley. Physiography. (Very valuable).	1 80	42
A. Irving. A Short Manual of Heat.	75	40
Fleeming Jenkin. Electricity and Magnetism.	1 50	29
A. M. Mayer. *Sound, $1.00 ; *Light.	1 00	29
C. W. MacCord. Kinematics of Machines.	5 00	50
J. C. Maxwell. *Theory of Heat.	1 50	29
Electricity and Magnetism. Oxford Clarendon Press. 2 vols.	8 00	42
T. C. Mendenhall. A Century of Electricity.	1 25	19
Thos. Nolan. *The Telescope.	50	48
R. H. Scott. *Elementary Meteorology.	—	79
*Weather-Charts and Storm-Warnings.	2 00	40
B. Silliman. *Principles of Physics.	3 10	39
Balfour Stewart. *Conservation of Energy.	1 50	29
Physics.	45	29
S. B. Thompson. Elementary Lessons in Electricity.	1 25	42

PHYSICS—*Cont'd.*				Price.	Pub's No.
J. Tyndall. *Molecular Physics.	.	.	.	$5 00	29
*Heat as a Mode of Motion.	.	.	.	2 50	29
*Lessons in Electricity.	.	.	.	I 00	29
*Light and Electricity.	.	.	.	I 25	29
*Light.	.	.	.	I 50	29
*Sound.	.	.	.	2 00	29
*Modern Meteorology.	.	.	.	I 50	48

[N.B.—In Physics, Silliman and Ganot are both good text-books, but Daniell represents much better, for advanced students, the style of modern thought on this subject. In Electricity, the small work of Thompson is an excellent introduction ; that of Clerk Maxwell is suitable for advanced students.]

MICROSCOPY.

	Price.	Pub's No.
Lionel S. Beale. *How to Work with the Microscope.	$7 50	42
E. Bausch. Manipulation of the Microscope.	50	53
J. W. Behrens. The Microscope in Botany. Translated by Hervey.	5 00	26
W. B. Carpenter. *The Microscope and its Revelations.	5 50	42
L. L. Clark. *Objects for the Microscope.	I 75	48
M. C. Cooke Ponds and Ditches.	75	49
One Thousand Objects for the Microscope.	50	49
C. S. Dolley. Technology of Bacteria.	2 00	26
Frey. The Microscope. Translated by Cutler. 1880.	4 25	51
P. H. Gosse. Evenings at the Microscope.	I 50	29
J. W. Griffith and A. Henfrey. *Micrographic Dictionary.	20 00	75
Jabez Hogg. *The Microscope.	3 50	46
C. T. Hudson and P. H. Gosse. *The Rotifera or Wheel-Animalcules. 2 vols.	24 00	40
F. L. James, M.D. Elementary Microscopical Technology.	50	79
C. Henry Kain. Reproduction of Schmidt's Atlas of Diatoms.	7 50	79
Lee. Microtomist's Vade Mecum.	3 00	71
W. P. Manton. Beginnings with the Microscope.	50	20

MICROSCOPY—*Cont'd.*	Price.	*Pub's No.*
J. Mayall, Jr. Lectures on the Microscope. 1886.	$0 80	63
Poulsen's Botanical Micro-Chemistry. Translated.	1 00	26
H. J. Slack. *Marvels of Pond Life.	1 75	70
J. E. Smith. How to See with the Microscope.	2 00	5
G. M. Sternberg. Photo-Micrographs and How to Make Them.	3 00	21
Alfred S. Stokes. Microscopy for Beginners.	1 50	36
Mary Treat, S. Wells, and F. L. Sargent. Through a Microscope.	55	7
C. O. Whitman. Microscopical Anatomy and Embryology. 1885.	3 00	26
J. G. Wood. Common Objects for the Microscope.	50	46
American Monthly Microscopical Journal, Washington, D. C.	—	—
The Microscope, Microscope Co., Detroit, Mich.	—	—
Monthly Microscopical Journal. 1869–1877. Discontinued.	—	—
Quarterly Journal Microscopical Science, London.	—	—
Journal Royal Microscopical Society, London. From 1878.	—	—

[N.B.—The best general book on the Microscope is Carpenter. James gives the complete history of a slide according to the most recent modes of mounting. Behrens is very complete for the botanical student, and Frey and Beale equally so for the medical.]

DIVISION II.

BOTANY.

Class I.—Structural Botany.

M. J. Berkeley. *Cryptogamic Botany.	—	68
C. E. Bessey. Botany for High Schools.	$1 35	38
G. L. Goodale. Physiological Botany.	2 30	39
Asa Gray. Structural and Systematic Botany.	2 30	39
—— Sachs. Text-book of Botany. Translated by Bennett and Dyer. 1875.	—	42
O. W. Thoné. Structural and Physiological Botany. Translated by Bennett. 1877.	—	50

Class II.—Classification, etc.	*Price.*	*Pub's No.*
Henry Baldwin. *The Orchids of New England.	$2 50	50
Bentham and Hooker. Genera Plantarum. 2 vols. 1862.	—	42
James Britten, F.L.S. *European Ferns : their Form, Habit and Culture. Colored Illustrations from Nature by D. Blair.	7 50	32
M. C. Cooke. Hand-book of British Fungi. 1871. Scarce.	—	42
A. W. Chapman. Flora of the Southern States. 1872.	2 50	39
J. M. Coulter. Botany of the Rocky Mountains.	2 50	39
A. De Candolle. *Prodromus Systematis Naturalis Regni Vegetabilis. 17 vols. 1824–1873.	—	79
W. G. Farlow. *Marine Algæ of New England.	1 50	26
Asa Gray. Manual of the Botany of the Northern United States. 1878.	2 50	39
Synoptical Flora of North America. 2 vols. Each.	5 00	39
—— Harvey. Nereis Borealis Americana.	—	4
Sir W. J. Hooker. Flora Borealis Americana.	—	45
Every Known Fern. 1868.	11 00	45
L. Lesquereux and T. P. James. *Manual of the Mosses of North America.	4 50	26
W. S. Sullivant. Musci and Hepaticæ of United States. 1866.	—	26
H. Tuckermann. Lichens of North America.	3 50	26
L. M. Underwood. Hepaticæ of North America.	1 50	26
A. Wood. Class-book of Botany. 1855.	3 50	30
H. C. Wood. Fresh Water Algæ of N. America.	7 50	45
F. Wolle. Fresh Water Algæ of United States. 2 vols. 1887.	10 00	56
Desmids of United States. 1886.	5 00	56
Botany of Geological Survey of California. 2 vols. 1880. Each.	5 00	79

Class III.—General Works.

W. W. Bailey. Collector's Hand-book.	1 50	13
M. C. Cooke. Microscopic Fungi.	2 00	70
*Rust, Smut, Mildew and Mould.	1 00	70
A. De Candolle. History of Cultivated Plants.	2 00	29

BOTANY—*Cont'd.*	Price.	Pub's No.
G. L. Goodale. A Few Common Plants.	$0 25	18
Asa Gray. How Plants Grow.	1 00	39
School and Field Botany.	2 10	39
Gertrude E. Hale. Little Flower People.	50	67
F. B. Hough. Elements of Forestry.	2 00	54
A. A. Knight. A Primer of Botany.	35	67
W. P. Manton. Field Botany.	50	20
D. P. Penhallow. Vegetable Histology.	1 00	79
H. Willey. Introduction to the Study of Lichens	1 00	79
O. R. Willis. Flora of New Jersey.	1 00	30
A. Wood. American Botanist and Florist.	2 50	30
Wood and Steele. How to Study Plants.	2 50	30
E. A. Youmans. First Book of Botany.	75	29
Descriptive Botany.	1 40	29

Class IV.—*Popular and Æsthetic.*

	Price.	Pub's No.
L. H. Bailey. *Talks Afield about Plants and the Science of Plants.	1 00	19
Bentley and Trimen. Medicinal Plants. 5 vols.	£11 11s.	70
C. E. Bessey. Botanical Atlas. 2 vols.	$6 00	41
W. Boot. Illustrations of the Genus Carex.	—	79
D. C. Eaton. *Ferns of North America. 2 vols.	30 00	26
N. H. Eggleston. Hand-Book of Tree-planting.	75	29
G. L. Goodale. *American Wild Flowers.	15 00	26
Grant Allen. Vignettes from Nature.	15	34
*The Colors of Flowers.	1 00	42
S. B. Herrick. *Wonders of Plant-Life.	1 50	45
A. B. Hervey. *Sea-Mosses.	2 00	13
Marcus E. Jones. Ferns of the West.	30	66
J. Lubbock. Flowers, Fruits and Leaves.	1 25	42
Thomas Meehan. Native Flowers and Ferns of the United States. 3 vols. 1879.	17 00	24
Michaux and Nuttall. North American Sylva. 5 vols.	—	79
H. S. Miner. *Orchids.	10 00	20
E. M. Pendleton. Scientific Agriculture.	1 50	30
Wm. Rhind. Vegetable Kingdom.	—	77
J. Robinson. Ferns : Their Homes and Ours.	1 50	26
Alfred Smee. My Garden.	—	69
Edward Sprague. *Bulbs.	2 50	19
*Flowers for the Parlor and Garden.	2 50	19
*Garden Flowers: How to Cultivate Them.	2 50	19

BOTANY—*Cont'd.*	Price.	Pub's No.
Orchids.	$3 00	19
*Rhododendrons.	2 00	19
W. C. Strong. *Fruit Culture and the Laying Out and Management of a Country Home.	1 00	19
L. M. Underwood. Our Native Ferns.	1 50	13
Wild Flower Portfolio. Three series, each being a selection of 40 wild flowers, printed in chromo-lithography, and put up in two handsome boxes. 6 boxes in all. Each.	1 50	32
Wild Flowers of the Rocky Mountains. Portfolio. A selection of 24 of the finest wild flowers, from original water colors. In 12 to 15 colors. 3 boxes, 8 pl. in each box. Each.	1 50	32
Botanical Gazette, Crawfordsville, Ind. Per annum.	2 00	—
Bulletin Torrey Botanical Club, Columbia College, N. Y. City. Per annum.	1 00	—

[N.B. The classification given by Bentham and Hooker, in their 'Genera Plantarum,' is the one now accepted. Gray's Manual describes the plants east of the Mississippi and north of Virginia, Chapman's gives those of the Gulf States, and Coulter's, or the Botany of California, the west coast plants. In structural and physiological botany, Sache is recent and exhaustive, Thome is good and smaller, Bessey covers the entire field of plant-life in general. Smee's 'My Garden' shows how much there is to observe and find out in a very limited area. De Candolle's *Prodromus* contains, in Latin, a description of all known plants. In cryptogamic botany, the work of Berkeley is scarce but very good, Sachs and Bessey both include cryptogams in their structural books. The older editions of 'Gray's Manual' included both ferns and mosses, but the mosses are left out of the later editions. Cooke's Fungi applies almost as well to the United States as to England. Wolle's books on Desmids and Fresh Water Algæ take the place of all others on these subjects for the United States.]

MINERALOGY AND METALLURGY.

W. R. Balch. Mines, Miners and Mining Interests in the United States.	—	62
Hilary Baurman. *Systematic Mineralogy.	$2 25	29
G. J. Brush. Manual of Determinative Mineralogy and Blowpipe Analysis.	3 50	50

MINERALOGY AND METALLURGY—*Cont'd.*	Price.	Pub's No.
S. M. Burnham. Precious Stones in Nature, Art and Literature.	$3 50	26
History and Uses of Limestones and Marbles.	6 00	26
A. H. Chester. A Catalogue of Minerals.	1 25	50
Crookes and Rohrig. A Practical Treatise on Metallurgy. 3 vols.	—	40
J. H. Collins. First Book of Mineralogy.	75	45
W. O. Crosby. Tables for the Determination of Common Minerals.	1 25	16
H. B. Cornwall. *Blowpipe Analysis.	2 50	48
E. S. Dana. Text-book of Mineralogy.	3 50	50
J. D. Dana. Descriptive Mineralogy.	10 00	50
Manual of Mineralogy.	2 00	50
W. Elderhorst. *Blowpipe Analysis.	2 50	64
I. C. Foye. *Hand-book of U. S. Minerals.	50	79
H. P. Gurney. *Crystallography.	50	44
G. G. Gore. *The Art of Electro-Metallurgy.	2 25	29
J. B. Jordan. *Elementary Crystallography (Valuable).	1 50	72
C. W. King. Antique Gems and Rings. 2 vols.	—	69
A. G. Lock. *Gold : Its Occurrence, etc.	20 00	79
E. H. Richards. First Lessons in Minerals.	10	18
W. A. Ross. *Blowpipe Analysis.	4 00	48
Hussak Smith. Instructions for the Determination of Rock-forming Minerals. 103 plates.	2 00	50
J. Swank. *Iron in All Ages.	—	79
E. H. Williams. A Manual of Lithology.	1 25	50

See Reports and Bulletins Geologic Survey of United States, Washington, D. C., and the Surveys of Many States.

[N.B.—In Mineralogy, Dana, Brush, and Plattner are standard authors. In the determination of minerals, the microscope has within a few years been applied with wonderful success, but the only book yet written in English suitable for a text-book on this subject is Hussak. The principal one is in German by Prof. Henry Rosenbusch, called *Mikroskopische Physiographie.*]

ZOÖLOGY—*In General.*

W. B. Carpenter. *Comparative Zoölogy.	—	79
Buel P. Colton. Elementary Course in Practical Zoölogy.	$0 80	18

ZOÖLOGY—*Cont'd.*	*Price.*	*Pub's No.*
—— Claus (Sedgwick). Text-book of Zoölogy. (Standard.) 2 vols.	$8 00	42
C. Gegenbaur. Comparative Anatomy. Translated by Bell and Lancaster.	5 50	42
T. H. Huxley. The Crayfish. An Introduction to Zoölogy.	1 75	29
J. S. Kingsley. *Riverside Natural History. (Standard.) 6 vols.	36 00	19
A. M. Marshall and C. A. Hursh. Junior Course in Practical Zoölogy.	3 50	45
E. S. Morse. *First Book of Zoölogy.	1 00	29
A. S. Packard. *Zoölogy for High Schools.	3 00	38
J. D. Steele. *Fourteen Weeks in Zoölogy.	1 50	30
Sanborn Tenney. *Elements of Zoölogy.	1 85	39
Natural History of Animals.	1 40	39
*Manual of Zoölogy.	2 30	47
Andrew Wilson. Facts and Fictions of Zoölogy.	15	34

ZOÖLOGY.—*Special.*

1. *LOWER INVERTEBRATES—CONCHOLOGY.*

E. C. Agassiz. *First Lesson in Natural History.	$0 25	18
Alexander Agassiz. *Seaside Studies in Natural History.	3 00	19
W. K. Brooks. *Hand-book of Invertebrate Zoölogy.	3 00	26
Check-List. North American Shells.	25	4
J. A. Dana. *Corals and Coral Islands.	4 00	33
J. H. Emerton. *Life on the Seashore.	1 50	26
Structure and Habits of Spiders.	1 50	26
A. A. Gould. *Invertebrates of Massachusetts.	—	27
S. Haldeman. Fresh Water Univalve Mollusca.	25 00	65
N. M. Hentz. *Spiders of the United States.	3 00	26
Hudson and Gosse. The Rotifera, or Wheel-Animalcules.	24 00	40
Alpheus Hyatt. *Oyster, Clam, etc.	25	18
*Hydroids, Corals, etc.	20	18
*Sponges.	20	18
*Worms and Crustacea.	25	18
W. Saville Kent. A Manual of Infusoria. 3 vols.	25 00	70
Josiah Keep. *West Coast Shells.	1 50	79

ZOÖLOGY—*Cont'd.*	*Price.*	*Pub's No.*
D. Landsborough. *British Zoöphytes, or Coral-lines.	—	42
Isaac Lea. *Conchology. 3 vols., folio. (Scarce.)	—	79
Joseph Leidy. Fresh Water Rhigopods of North America.	—	79
M. Roberts. Popular History of Mollusca. .	—	42
E. B. Sowerby. *Popular British Conchology. .	—	42
G. B. Tryon. *Structural and Systematic Conchology. 3 vols.	$20 00	65
Cheap edition. 1 vol.	12 00	65
Manual of Conchology. (Now publishing.)	—	65
A. E. Verrill. *Invertebrates of Vineyard Sound.	3 00	—
S. P. Woodward. *Recent and Fossil Shells. .	—	42
Manual of Mollusca.	—	4

2. *INSECTS—ENTOMOLOGY.*

J. P. Ballard. *Insect Lives ; or, Born in Prison.	1 00	52
H. S. Conant. *Butterfly Hunters. . . .	1 50	79
E. T. Cresson. Synopsis of the Hymenoptera of North America, 1887.	3 00	57
P. M. Duncan. Transformations of Insects. .	2 00	32
A. J. Ebell. *Insects and How to Observe Them.	30	79
Canadian Entomologist. Monthly. . Per year.	1 00	—
Edwards. *Butterflies of North America. Series 1, $35.00 ; Series 2, $40.00 ; Series 3, in parts. . . . . . Each.	2 25	19
G. H. French. Butterflies of the Eastern United States.	2 00	61
T. W. Harris. *Insects Injurious to Vegetation. $4.00 and	6 50	41
H. A. Hazen. Synopsis of Neuroptera of North America.	—	4
John Lubbock. *Ants, Bees and Wasps. . .	2 00	29
Le Conte and Horn. Classification of the Coleoptera.	—	4
C. J. Maynard. *Butterflies of New England. .	7 00	26
J. G. Morris. Synopsis of the Lepidoptera of North America.	—	4
A. S. Packard, Jr. Guide to the Study of Insects.	5 00	38
William Saunders. Insects Injurious to Fruits. .	—	—
M. Van Beneden. Animal Parasites. . . .	1 50	29

ZOÖLOGY—Cont'd.	Price.	Pub's No.
S. H. Scudder. Butterflies: their Structure, Changes and Life Histories.	$3 00	38
Mary Treat. My Garden Pets. (Ants, Wasps, Spiders, etc.)	—	22
T. Say. *Entomology of North America. 2 vols.	15 00	—
J. G. Wood. *Insects at Home.	3 50	40
*Insects Abroad.	3 50	40
J. O. Westwood. Entomologist's Text-book.	37 50	42

[See for valuable notes on Economic Entomology, Reports and Bulletins of the United States Department of Agriculture, and Entomological Commission, Washington, D. C.]

ZOÖLOGY.

3. VERTEBRATES.

a. In general.

D. S. Jordan. Vertebrates of Northern United States.	$2 50	8
Manual of the Vertebrates.	2 50	8

b. Reptiles.

Samuel Garman. *Reptiles and Batrachians of North America.	4 00	54

c. Fish.

C. Girard. *Fresh Water Fish of North America.	1 50	4
Hugo Mulertt. *The Gold Fish and its Culture.	60	54
H. G. Seeley, F.R.S. *Fresh Water Fishes of Europe.	5 00	32
Various Government Publications:		

d. Birds.—Ornithology, Oölogy and Taxidermy.

J. J. Audubon. *Birds of America. 7 vols. (Scarce.)	—	—
Austin. *Taxidermy without a Teacher.	50	20
S. F. Baird. *Land Birds of California.	10 00	21
Baird, Brown and Ridgeway. *Birds of North America. Land Birds. 3 vols. $30.00; colored, $60.00; Water Birds, $24.00; colored.	60 00	21
T. Brown. *Manual of Taxidermy.	1 50	45
Elliott Coues. *Birds of the Northwest.	4 50	27
Check-List of Birds.	3 00	17
*Key to North American Birds, and Field Ornithology.	7 50	17

ZOÖLOGY—*Cont'd.*	*Price.*	*Pub's No.*
Elliot Coues and W. A. Stearns. *Bird-Life : A Manual of Ornithology.	$5 00	20
Geo. H. Holden. *Canaries and Cage-Birds. .	2 00	37
Ernest Ingersoll. *Birds'-Nesting. . . .	1 25	26
J. H. Langille. Our Birds in their Haunts. .	3 00	26
C. J. Maynard. Manual of Taxidermy. . .	1 25	26
Olive Thorne Miller. Bird-Ways. . . .	1 25	19
H. D. Minot. Land and Game Birds of New England.	3 00	26
R. Ridgeway. Manual of North American Birds.	7 50	61
Bradford Torrey. Birds in the Bush. . .	1 25	19
Alexander Wilson. *American Ornithology. According to style, . From $110.00 to	7 50	64
Wild Birds Portfolio. A selection of 40 beautifully Colored Plates of Familiar Wild Birds. Two handsome boxes. . . Each.	1 50	32
American Ornithologists' Union Check-List of North American Birds. . . .	3 00	—

  e. Mammals.

F. S. Buckland. *Log-book of a Zoölogist. .	3 00	61
Hartman. Anthropoid Apes. . . .	1 75	29
St. George Mivart. The Cat. 200 illustrations.	3 50	47

  f. Man—Archæology and Ethnology.

Abbott, C. C. *Primitive Industry of the Native Races of America.	3 00	23
American Journal of Archæology. . Per year.	5 00	81
ARCHÆOLOGICAL INSTITUTE PUBLICATIONS. .	—	11

 I. *School of Classical Studies at Athens.*
  a Bulletin I. (*All out in 1887.*)
  b Preliminary Report of an Archæological Journey in Asia Minor. Inscriptions.
  c *Papers I. (*All out in 1887.*)
  d *Report on Explorations at Assos, 1881. (*All out 1887.*)
 II. *American Series.*
  a *New Mexico.
  b *Tour in Mexico, 1881.
 III. *Reports.*

Bancroft. Native Races. 5 vols. . .	$22 50	2
Bureau of Ethnology. *Reports I.–IV. Each.	3 00	4
W. Boyd Dawkins. *Cave-Hunting. . .	6 00	42

ZOÖLOGY—*Cont'd.*	Price.	Pub's No.
De Mortillet. *L'Homme Préhistorique.*	5 francs.	78
J. W. Foster. *Prehistoric Races of the United States.	$3 00	6
C. C. Jones. Antiquities of the Southern Indians.	6 00	29
J. P. Maclean. The Mound-Builders.	1 00	54
Antiquity of Man.	60	54
O. T. Mason. Articles in *American Naturalist.*	—	—
M. de Nadaillac. Prehistoric America.	5 00	45
Peabody Museum of Ethnology. 21 Reports.	—	23
John F. Short. *North Americans of Antiquity. 8vo.	3 00	36
H. R. Schoolcraft. Algic Researches. Out of print, and very scarce at second-hand for about	3 00	—
H. R. Schoolcraft, *Archives of Aboriginal Knowledge. 6 vols., folio.	90 00	61

Smithsonian Institution. Miscellaneous Publications, commonly illustrated. For example :   4

	Price.	Smith. Inst. No.
Abbott. Stone Age in New Jersey.	$0 25	394
Boehmer. Index to Smith. Inst. Anthrop. Pub.	10	421
Bransford. Antiquity of Costa Rica.	10	619
" Archæological Researches in Nicaragua.	2 00	383
Cope. West India Bone Cave.	2 00	489
Dall. Remains of Later Prehistoric Man in Alaska Caves.	2 00	318
Desor. Palafittes of the Lake of Neuchatel.	10	360
Gibbs, Hardisty, Jones, Ross—Tinneh or Chepewyan Indians.	10	365
Gillman. Mound-Builders of Michigan.	20	393
Gore. Tuckahoe, or Indian Bread.	5	482
Haldeman. Polychrome Bead from Florida.	5	404
Henry. Circular on Archæology and Ethnology.	2	205
Henry. List of Photographic Portraits of Indians.	10	216
Howitt. Australian Group—Relations.	5	596
Jones. Aboriginal Structures in Georgia.	5	400
" Aboriginal Remains in Tennessee.	3 00	259
Keugla. Archæological Map of D. C.	5	537

SMITHSONIAN INSTITUTION PUBLICATIONS—*Cont'd.* Price. $\frac{\text{Smith.}}{\text{Inst. No.}}$

Knight. Savage Weapons at Philadelphia Exhibition.	$0 25	415
Lapham. Antiquities of Wisconsin.	10 00	70
Mason. Latimer Collection of Antiquities of Porto Rico.	5	397
Mason. Miscellaneous Anthropological Papers, 1879.	10	420
Mason. Miscellaneous Anthropological Papers, 1881.	10	481
Rau. Flint Implements Found in Illinois.	5	370
" Drilling Stone without Metal.	5	372
" Gold Ornaments from Mounds in Florida.	5	403
" Palenque Tablet.	2 00	331
" Stock-in-Trade of Aboriginal Lapidary.	5	402
Romer. Prehistorical Antiquities of Hungary.	2	392
Simpson. Coronado's March in Search of Cibola.	5	561
Squier. Aboriginal Monuments of New York.	6 00	15
Swan. Haidah Indians.	2 00	267
Trans. Anthropol. Institution of Washington. Vol. I., 1879–1882.	1 00	501
Trans. Anthropol. Institution of Washington. Abstract. 1879–1880.	1 00	502
Trans. Anthropol. Institution of Washington. Vol. II., 1882–1888.	1 00	544
Thomas. Directions for Mound Exploration.	2	601

g. *Guides.*

Louis Agassiz. *Methods of Study.	1 50	19
H. H. Ballard. Hand-book of the Agassiz Association.	75	52
H. D. Butler. Family Aquarium.	75	34
J. S. Kingsley. Naturalists' Assistant.	1 50	26
C. T. Maynard. Naturalists' Guide.	2 00	26

DIVISION III.

NATURAL HISTORY.—*Popular.*

F. Albertsen. *Four-footed Lovers.	1 00	20
A. B. Buckley. *Life and Her Children.	1 50	29
Winners in Life's Race.	1 50	29
P. A. Chadbourne. Lectures.	75	30

NATURAL HISTORY—*Cont'd.*	Price.	Pub's No.
Cecil's *Natural History.	$0 85	28
Sarah Cooper. Animal Life in the Sea and on the Land.	1 50	36
Ernst Haeckel. A Visit to Ceylon.	1 75	—
A. B. Harris. Door-Yard Folks.	1 00	22
J. Hinton. *Life in Nature.	15	34
C. F. Holder. *Living Lights.	2 00	32
W. Hooker, *Child's Book of Nature. 3 parts. No. 1, 60c.; 2 and 3, each, 65c.; bound in one.	1 60	36
Ernest Ingersoll. Old Ocean.	1 00	22
*Habits of Animals.	75	7
J. Johonnot. Glimpses of the Animate World.	1 20	29
H. C. McCook. Tenants of an Old Farm.	2 50	35
McGUFFEY'S NATURAL HISTORY READERS:		
1. Familiar Animals and their Wild Kindred.	58	55
2. Living Creatures of Water, Land and Air.	58	55
Gilbert White. Selborne.	75	36
J. G. Wood. Popular Natural History. 500 Illustrations.	1 75	64
Homes Without Hands.	4 50	36
*Strange Dwellings.	1 75	40
*Out of Doors.	1 75	40
*Bible Animals.	3 50	40
*The Branch Builders.	1 00	40
*Wonderful Nests.	1 25	40
*Homes Underground.	1 25	40

MISCELLANEOUS.

	Price	Pub's No.
—— Abercrombie. Weather.	1 75	29
Louis Agassiz. *Journey in Brazil.	2 50	19
*His Life and Correspondence. By E. C. Agassiz. 2 vols.	4 00	19
Francis Bacon. Novum Organum and Advancement of Learning.	2 00	47
H. W. Bates. *Naturalist on the Amazons.	2 50	25
Mary E. Bamford. The Look-About Club.	1 50	22
My Land and Water Friends.	1 50	22
Mrs. Boyle. Days and Hours in a Garden.	2 00	25
J. Bernstein. The Five Senses.	1 75	29
C. L. Brightwell. Lives of Labor.	1 25	79

MISCELLANEOUS—*Cont'd.*	Price.	Pub's No.
John Burroughs. Birds and Poets.	$1 50	19
*Wake Robin.	1 50	19
Winter Sunshine.	1 50	19
Locusts and Wild Honey.	1 50	19
Pepacton and other Sketches.	1 50	19
Fresh Fields.	1 50	19
Signs and Seasons.	1 50	19
A. B. Buckley. *The Fairyland of Science.	1 50	29
H. J. Clark. *Mind in Nature.	3 50	29
J. W. Draper. The Conflict Between Religion and Science.	1 75	29
G. F. Figuier. *The Human Race.	4 50	29
*Primitive Man.	3 00	32
*The World Before the Deluge.	1 50	29
*The Ocean World.	1 50	32
*Birds and Reptiles.	1 50	32
*The Vegetable World.	1 50	32
John Fiske. Excursions of an Evolutionist.	2 00	19
Mrs. Alfred Gatty. *Parables from Nature.	75	31
L. Grindon. Life : Its Nature and Varieties.	2 25	61
Plant Life.	1 00	14
Emblems.	1 00	14
Sexuality of Nature.	1 00	14
Trees of Old England.	1 00	14
C. Hartwig. *The Sea and its Living Wonders.	3 50	40
*The Tropical World.	3 50	40
*The Polar World.	3 50	40
*The Subterranean World.	3 50	40
*The Aerial World.	3 00	29
*Sea Monsters and Sea Birds.	1 00	40
*Denizens of the Deep.	1 00	40
*Volcanoes and Earthquakes.	1 00	40
C. F. Holder. *Marvels of Animal Life.	2 00	47
W. Houghton. *Country Walks of a Naturalist with his Children.	—	79
P. H. Gosse. Romance of Natural History.	2 00	61
A. Humboldt. Kosmos. 3 vols. (Bohn's library)	—	29
Views of Nature.	—	29
T. H. Huxley. Darwin and Humboldt.	15	34
Ernest Ingersoll. *Friends Worth Knowing.	1 00	36
*Old Ocean.	1 00	7
R. Jeffries. *Wild Life in a Southern Country	1 75	25

MISCELLANEOUS—*Cont'd.*	Price.	Pub's No.
Dr. D. S. Jordan. Science Sketches.	$1 50	8
A. Karr. Around in My Garden.	—	79
J. Le Conte. Sight.	1 50	29
G. P. Marsh. The Earth as Modified by Human Actions.	3 50	47
J. Michelet. The Bird.	4 00	80
The Ocean World.	—	80
The Desert.	—	80
The World Before the Deluge.	—	80
John Milne. Earthquakes.	1 75	29
R. Mudie. Observations of Nature	75	36
Maurice Noel. Buz.	1 00	38
H. O. Oersted. Spirit in Nature. (Bohn's Library.)	—	79
F. Papillon. *Nature and Life.	2 00	29
*A World of Wonders.	2 00	29
J. Patton. Natural Resources of the United States.	3 00	29
J. B. Pettigrew. Animal Locomotion.	1 75	29
F. A. Pouchet. *The Universe.	8 00	47
T. L. Phipson. *Utilization of Minute Life.	—	42
E. P. Roe. Nature's Serial Story.	1 50	33
—— Roberts. Rules of Order.	75	36
F. B. Sanborn. Life of H. D. Thoreau.	1 25	19
Samuel Smiles. *Scotch Naturalist.	1 50	36
*Robert Dick.	1 50	36
Maurice Thompson. Byways and Bird Notes.	60	28
D. Thoreau. Walden ; or, Life in the Woods.	1 50	19
A Week on the Concord and Merrimac Rivers.	1 50	19
Excursions in Field and Forest.	1 50	19
The Maine Woods.	1 50	19
Cape Cod.	1 50	19
Early Spring in Massachusetts.	1 50	19
J. Tyndall. Faraday as a Discoverer.	1 00	29
Science for Unscientific People.	2 50	29
Belfast Address.	50	29
Mrs. Ware. Thoughts in My Garden.	—	29
C. D. Warner. In the Wilderness.	75	19
The Naturalists' Directory : containing an alphabetical list of nearly all the leading naturalists, with their specialties and addresses.	—	15

MISCELLANEOUS—*Cont'd.*   Price.   Pub's No.

Herbarium—Ballard, H. H., and Thayer, S. P.
 For the convenient preservation of flowers,
 ferns and leaves. Contains directions for
 collecting and preserving plants; blanks
 for an analytical record of each specimen,
 pages for mounting plants, and gummed
 paper to fasten them. $1 50   12
J. G. Wood. Nature's Teaching. Human In-
 vention Anticipated by Nature.   .   .   2 50   25

AN INDEX OF INDEXES.

The young student may begin with the conviction that something of value has been written about everything, if it can only be
found. To find it is the difficulty, and to overcome this difficulty
so many indexes of different kinds have been made, that now the
student needs a catalogue of indexes. It is true that those boys
and girls who live in the country, away from large cities where the
large libraries are, find it very difficult to get hold of the books
they need, even when they know their names. Quite likely some
of the Agassiz Chapters might make an arrangement such as they
have in Australia, where the great libraries in Melbourne and the
other large cities have a branch office in each of the little towns
for hundreds of miles around, and send boxes, made for the purpose and filled with the books called for, every week or two weeks,
to these towns by rail, so that the country people have almost as
much good of the big libraries as those people who live in cities.
Of course they contribute to the big library some money, but they
have a great many more books to select from than if the same
money was spent on a little home town library.

SOME OF THESE INDEXES ARE:

Index to Periodical Literature. By W. F. Poole. Boston:
 Osgood & Co., 1882.
Catalogue of Scientific Papers. Royal Society of London: Trüb-
 ner & Co., 1879. Continued. 8 vols.
Dictionary of English Literature. S. A. Allibone. Philadelphia:
 Childs & Peterson, 1859.
Reports of Committee on Indexing Chemical Literature. See
 Yearly Reports of American Association Advancement of
 Science.

Thesaurus Literaturæ Botanicæ. Pritzel. Brockhaus. Leipzig:
  1872. Modified, somewhat enlarged, and republished as
  Guide to the Literature of Botany. By Benjamin Daydon
  Jackson. London: Longmans, Green & Co., 1881.
  These works contain the names of all books on botany.
Descriptive Catalogue of the Government publications of the
  United States. B. P. Poore, 1774 to 1881. Government
  Printing Office, Washington.
Nomenclator Fungorum. J. A. Streinz. Supplement to 1863.
Nomenclator Botanicus. E. D. Steudel. Second Edition, 1841.
Synonymiæ Botanicæ. L. Pfeiffer, 1870–1874.
Bibliographical Index to North American Botany. Serano
  Watson.
Smithsonian Contributions. XV. 1878–1880.

[Members of the A. A., desiring more special information regarding any book, may address Mr. O. Bjerregaard, librarian of the
Astor Library, N. Y. City, who has most generously volunteered
to place his invaluable experience at the service of those who
require such assistance.]

PUBLISHERS' OR AUTHORS' ADDRESSES.

 1. The Bancroft Co., .   History Building, San Francisco, Cal.
 2. The History Co., .   "   "
 3. Director U. S. Geological Survey, .   Washington, D. C.
 4. Smithsonian Institution,   .   .   "
 5. Duncan Bros.,   .   .   .   56 State St., Chicago, Ill.
 6. S. C. Griggs & Co.,   .   87 Wabash Ave.,   "
 7. The Interstate Publishing Co.,   .   .   .   "
 8. A. C. McClurg & Co., ...   "
 9. Clifford Mitchell, M.D., ...   "
10. J. P. Morton & Co.,   .   .   .   Louisville, Ky.
11. Archæological Institute, ... Salem, Mass.
12. H. H. Ballard, ...   Pittsfield, Mass.
13. E. A. Bates, ... Salem, Mass.
14. H. H. Carter & Karrick,   .   .   .   Boston, Mass.
15. S. E. Cassino,   .   .   . 137 High St.,   "
16. W. O. Crosby, care Boston Soc. of Nat. History, Boston, Mass.
17. Estes & Lauriat, ...   "
18. D. C. Heath & Co., ...   "
19. Houghton, Mifflin & Co., ...   "
20. Lee & Shepard, ...   "
21. Little, Brown & Co., ...   "
22. D. Lothrop & Co., ...   "

23. Peabody Museum of Ethnology, . . Cambridge, Mass.
24. L. Prang & Co., ... Boston, Mass.
25. Roberts Brothers, ... "
26. Bradlee Whidden, ... "
27. Wright & Potter, . 18 Post Office Square, "
28. John B. Alden, . . . 393 Pearl St., New York.
29. D. Appleton & Co., ... "
30. A. S. Barnes & Co., ... "
31. Robert Carter & Bros., . . 530 Broadway, "
32. Cassell & Co., ... "
33. Dodd, Mead & Co., ... "
34. Jos. Fitzgerald, . . 108 Chambers St., "
35. Fords, Howard & Hurlbert, ... "
36. Harper & Brothers, ... "
37. Geo. H. Holden, . . . 240 Sixth Ave., "
38. Henry Holt & Co., ... "
39. Ivison, Blakeman & Co., ... "
40. Longmans, Green & Co., 15 East Sixteenth St., "
41. Orange Judd Company, ... "
42. Macmillan & Co., ... New York.
43. Phillips & Hunt, . . . 805 Broadway, "
44. E. & J. B. Young & Co., ... "
45. G. P. Putnam's Sons, ... "
46. George Routledge & Sons, 9 Lafayette Place, "
47. Charles Scribner's Sons, ... "
48. D. Van Nostrand, ... "
49. Frederick Warne & Co., 20 Lafayette Place, "
50. John Wiley & Sons, . . 15 Astor Place, "
51. William Wood & Co., . 27 Great Jones Street, "
52. The Writers' Publishing Co., 21 University Place, "
53. Bausch & Lomb, ... Rochester, N. Y.
54. Robert Clarke & Co., ... Cincinnati, O.
55. Van Antwerp, Bragg & Co., . . . "
56. F. Wolle, ... Bethlehem, Pa.
57. American Entomological Society, . . Philadelphia, Pa.
58. H. Carey Baird & Co., 810 Walnut Street, "
59. P. Blakiston, Son & Co., . . . "
60. Lea Brothers & Co., ... "
61. J. B. Lippincott Company, . . . "
62. Mining Industrial Pub. Co., . . . "
63. Jas. W. Queen & Co., ... "
64. Porter & Coates, ... "
65. G. W. Tryon, ... "
66. Dr. Marcus E. Jones, . . . Salt Lake City, Utah.

67. Ginn & Co., ... Boston, Mass.
68. H. Balliere & Co., ... London, Eng.
69. George Bell & Sons, ... "
70. David Bogue & Co., ... "
71. J. & A. Churchill, ... "
72. Thomas Murby, ... "
73. Sonnenschein, Lowery & Co., . . . "
74. Trübner & Co., ... "
75. J. Van Voorst, ... "
76. William Blackwood & Sons, . . Edinburgh, Scotland.
77. Blackie & Son, ... Glasgow, "
78. Rheinwald, ... Paris, France.
79. The Baker & Taylor Co., ... New York.
80. Thos. Nelson & Sons, ... "
81. A. L. Frothingham, ... Princeton, N. J.

NOTE.—Where the publisher is unknown or uncertain in the foregoing list, the address of The Baker & Taylor Co., Booksellers, New York (No. 79 in the list), is given, as the books can always be obtained through them.

CHAPTER XVI.

NOTES.

IT may be useful to give here a few notes that have been made by members of the A. A., partly to show what sort of work is being done, and partly to furnish a suggestion to new members of what they can do. These notes, as well as most of the letters from chapters and friends already given, are taken nearly at random from our monthly reports that have appeared in *The Swiss Cross.* Those wishing a full knowledge of our work, must refer to the numbers of that magazine since January, 1887.

BIRDS OF PICTOU, NOVA SCOTIA.

I send you a list of the birds which I found and identified last year in Pictou. I found them all, the duck excepted, within a space of not more than thirty acres around Cliff Cottage.

WILLIE SHERATON, Cor. Mem. Chapter 1.

STRAY PELICANS.

A neighbor was out with a lantern on every dark and foggy evening, when several pelicans flew against him, nearly knocking him over. They were evidently lost, and so bewildered that eight of them were easily captured, and, even then, the remainder of the large flock would not leave so long as the light was visible. I think they were the common white American pelican.

JESSE FRENCH, Sec. Chapter 432,
Grand Rapids, La Moure Co., Dakota.

BEES AND PETUNIAS.

After watching bumble-bees for the whole summer, I have never yet seen one enter the tube of the petunia. Instead of this they puncture the wall of the corolla at a point in the angle formed between it and the calyx, insert their proboscides, and extract the honey.

GILBERT VAN INGEN.

HOME-BREWED SNOW-STORM.

I can testify to the following, which took place in the kitchen on wash-day. It was near Richmond, Ind. The temperature was about 15° below zero. While the room was misty from the vapor from tubs and boilers, the outside door was opened. A shaft of cold air struck across the room, and its course was distinctly marked by a dense swarm of well-defined snow-flakes, which fell rapidly to the floor. We repeated the experiment for the sake of seeing a ' home-brewed ' snow-storm.

JOSEPH MOORE.

EFFECT OF AN EARTHQUAKE ON INSECTS.

On the night of August 31, 1886, when the first tremor was felt by members of our family, the music of hundreds of katydids, crickets, and other insects among the pines, suddenly ceased, and did not begin again until after the shocks (which continued about an hour) had ceased. The stars shone in a cloudless sky, no wind was blowing, and an oppressive silence covered the land. No sound was heard, with the exception of howling dogs and the cries of frightened negroes.

CARRIE H. GLOSSER,
Morganton, N. C., Sec. Chapter II.

MUSKRATS AND MUSSEL-SHELLS.

Having driven a muskrat into the water, I found a mussel which it seemed to have dropped. It was not open, but had one valve partially broken at one end. I broke the ice and found a large pile of shells just under the bank. These shells had one valve whole, and the other broken, at the places where the cords are that hold the valves together.

ROGER C. ADAMS, Pres. 955.

I have watched muskrats by the hour : have seen them go into the water, come up on a log or stone with a clam, sit down on their haunches, take the clam between their fore-feet, and pull the shell open far enough to insert their noses and extract the mussel.

D. A. KINNEY, Pres. 565.

FLOWER-TRAPS.

Look at the tempting pea-blossoms of *Desmodium acuminatus*, or ' beggar's ticks.' A fly alights upon the small pink flower, when lo ! it seems to explode, and the insect is greeted with a blinding cloud of dust. This is a trap so delicately set, that, at the lightest touch, the spring, consisting of a rigid column of filaments enclosing the young pod, is released from the overlapping petals, and the anthers shower the intruder with pollen. But this pollen-shower is an innocent joke compared with the trap of *Apocynum androsæmifolium*, or ' dog-bane.' Let a fly but thrust its tongue into a flower, and the stamens instantly fasten on its tip, holding the fly in a grip from which it seldom, if ever, escapes alive.

THEODORE KELLOGG, De Pere, Wis.

FROGS AT HOME IN WINTER.

Some of the readers of these reports may have been puzzled to know where all the frogs came from last spring, almost before the frost was out of the ground. They all seemed well, and able to sing ; and in no way did they appear to have suffered from the cold weather. I am often obliged, during the winter months, to secure the assistance of a frog to make the fact of blood-circulation plain to my students in zoölogy, and, as I do not always have a supply of frogs on hand, I have many times gone to their winter homes and taken them out of their comfortable quarters for a course in the laboratory. A spring is selected, which contains as many stones, sticks, leaves, and as much mud, as possible, and a regular attack upon the inhabitants is at once commenced. I first dig a ditch to drain off the water, and then I remove carefully the sticks and stones, watching all the time for signs of life under each piece ; and afterward I dig down into the mud, usually with my hands, to avoid hurting the animals which may be buried in it. I have never failed to catch several frogs, cray-fish, newts, worms, and sometimes minnows and smaller animals, fit for winter study. I have always been repaid for my trouble by the enthusiasm with which three or four students—who volunteered to help me—dig in the mud after the specimens, and by the interest they take in learning how a frog passes a cold winter in north-western Pennsylvania, at an altitude of twelve hundred feet above the sea, when the temperature is often twenty degrees below zero, and the ground frozen from three to five feet deep. Of course large numbers of these animals winter in swamps, though we cannot find them there, but we may always be sure of our game if we choose a living spring.
J. H. MONTGOMERY.

LINGULÆ.

Chinese boys go on mud sleds, and dig, at low tide, from the sandy shores of the Swatow Bay, great basketfuls of *lingulæ*, tiny mollusks with thin, green, horny, oblong shells. The *lingula* is found in beds, and is often buried in the muddy sand to a depth of ten inches. It is usually attached to a little stone by a muscular pedicel, and by the extension and contraction of its pedicel it enjoys feeding in clear water at high tide, and napping in sandy depths at low tide. Unlike the clam, which has its two shell-valves on its two sides, like a garment that opens before and behind, this little shell-fish has its two shell-valves on its back and front, like a garment that opens at the sides. Moreover, it is one of the very few kinds of living creatures that have existed unchanged from the earliest geological times. Before there were men, or sheep, or frogs, or trout, there were *lingulæ ;* and this brave little tribe has held its place and perpetuated itself in the world, through many changes of climate and circumstance. But, although it is of so ancient race, it is not intellectually superior to other shell-fish, and should serve as a warning to us against pride of pedigree. The Chinese, who are mere upstarts in comparison with it, sell it in the market at three cents a pound, fry it in lard, and eat it as a relish with their rice.

ADELE M. FIELDE, Swatow, China.

A WOODPECKER'S SUGAR-BUSH.

I have detected one of our yellow-bellied woodpeckers, *Picus varius*, tapping a maple-tree for the sake of the sap. Attracted to my window by a vigorous hammering, I saw a beautiful male bird sinking a shaft near the base of a large maple. It struck me as being a discouraging place to bore for grubs, as the tree was healthy and the sounds from the tapping gave no evidence of hollowness ; so I thought at first it might be a case of misguided instinct, or perhaps merely an experimental bore. As soon as one hole was completed another was begun, and by the time that was done the sap had commenced to flow freely from the first. It was then I noticed that it was the sweet sap the fellow was after, and not with the hope of any other reward that the bore was made, for, as the sap flowed, it was sipped up, first from the first hole and then from the second, and meanwhile, between drinks, the little fellow was vigorously at work upon a third excavation. When this was done, and all three taps flowing profusely, his sweet tongue was not yet sated, but his scarlet head was kept bobbing to and fro, sipping the sap from the three holes, while he energetically started a fourth. This completed, and all four taps well under way, his whole attention was for a few moments devoted to his sugar-bush, until, at length satisfied, he flew off— possibly to get a pickle !

J. W. CLARK, Albany, N. Y.

CHAPTER XVII.

The Council of the A. A.

We take extreme pleasure in presenting a revised list of the names and addresses of the gentlemen who have volunteered their services to our Association. These specialists are willing to answer questions and determine specimens in their several departments for any member of the Association. Many of them have been connected with us in this helpful capacity for several years, and as all such, in now renewing their previous gracious offer of assistance, have deplored the small number of requests for assistance they have received, instead of complaining of too frequent applications, our members may feel that they cannot compliment our friends more highly than by freely bringing to them for solution whatever difficulties may perplex them.

ARCHÆOLOGY.

Hilborne T. Cresson, 224 S. Broad St., Philadelphia, Penn.

Mr. Joseph Wigglesworth, Wilmington, Del.

BIBLIOGRAPHY.

O. Bjerregaard, the Astor Library, New York, N. Y.

BOTANY.

Dr. A. W. Chapman [*Southern Flora*], Appalachicola, Florida.

Marcus E. Jones, A.M. [*Plants west of the Mississippi*], W. 3d S. Street, Salt Lake City, Utah.

C. R. Orcutt [*Pacific Coast*], San Diego, Cal.

F. Leroy Sargent [*Lichens*], University of Wisconsin, Madison, Wis.

W. H. Seaman, M.D., 1424 Eleventh St., Washington, D. C.

Prof. William Trelease, Shaw School of Botany, St. Louis, Mo.

Prof. W. Whitman Bailey, 6 Cushing St., Providence, R. I.

CHEMISTRY.

Peter Collier, Washington, D. C.

Prof. William Frear [*Agricultural Chemistry*], State College, Penn.

C. J. Lincoln, Aspinwall Hill, Brookline, Mass.

S. P. Sharples, State Assayer, 13 Broad St., Boston, Mass.

A. J. Sherman, 308 Walnut St., Chicago, Ill.

Prof. Charles S. Doggett, Walpole, Mass.

CONCHOLOGY.

Harry E. Dore, Portland, Oregon.

Thomas Morgan, Box 164, Somerville, N. J.

Andrew Nichols, Jr., Asylum Station, Mass.

C. R. Orcutt [*Pacific Coast*], San Diego, Cal.

G. H. Parker, Divinity Hall, Cambridge, Mass.

Prof. D. Bruce Richards, 1726 N. 18th St., Philadelphia, Penn.

ENTOMOLOGY.

H. F. Bassett [*Gall-Flies*], Silas Bronson Library, Waterbury, Conn.

A. W. Putnam-Cramer [*Lepidoptera*], 308 Macon St., Brooklyn, N. Y.

Prof. C. H. Fernald [*Small Moths*], Amherst, Mass.

Prof. Leland O. Howard, Dept. Agr., Division of Entomology, Washington, D. C.

J. A. Lintner, Office of State Entomologist, Albany, N. Y.

GEOLOGY.

Prof. Le Roy F. Griffin, Lake Forest Univ., Lake Forest, Ill.

W. R. Lighton, 112 S. Esplanade, Leavenworth, Kan.

Chas. F. Prosser [*Devonian Fossils*], Cornell Univ., Ithaca, N. Y.

Prof. C. R. Van Hise, Dept. of the Interior, Geological Survey, Madison, Wis.

MICROSCOPY.

H. F. Atwood, Esq., Rochester-German Insurance Co., Rochester, N. Y.

Robert W. Wood, Jr., Revere St., Jamaica Plain, Mass.

MINERALOGY.

Prof. O. W. Crosby, Bost. Soc. Nat. Hist., Boston, Mass.

Prof. Thomas Egleston, Columbia College, New York, N. Y.

Prof. S. F. Peckham, Bristol, R. I.

Prof. F. W. Stæbner, Normal School, Westfield, Mass.

Frank W. Traphagen, Ph.D. [*Chemical Analysis*], Lock Box 135, Staunton, Va.

ORNITHOLOGY AND OÖLOGY.

J. de B. Abbott, M.D., Box 230, Bristol, Penn.

Amos W. Butler, Acad. of Sc., Brookville, Ind.

Arthur P. Chadbourne, Brattle St., Cambridge, Mass.

D. H. Eaton, Box 1235, Woburn, Mass.

Geo. Bird Grinnell, Ph.D., 37 Park Row, New York, N. Y.

PHYSIOLOGY.

Wm. M. Baird, M.D., Washington, N. J.

ZOÖLOGY.

C. F. Holder [*General Biology*], Pasadena, Cal.
David S. Jordan [*Fish*], Bloomington, Ind.
Geo. W. Peckham [*Spiders*], High School, Milwaukee, Wis.

These gentlemen can hardly realize how great a service they are rendering. There are thousands of young and older amateur naturalists belonging to our society, most of whom, living in remote towns, have few opportunities of instruction in the subject of their choice. They are now placed in such a position that they can go on with their observations without leaving home; can be advised as to the best books for consultation in their several departments ; can exchange specimens and thoughts with members in all the different States and Territories ; and can have the assistance of men trained in special departments of science, and all without expense. May not the A. A. be the means of solving one of the most perplexing educational questions of the day?

CONDITIONS OF CORRESPONDENCE.

The following rules must be strictly regarded not only in corresponding with the gentlemen just named, but also in addressing the President.

1. *Enclose in each letter, requiring an answer, a stamped and addressed envelope, or a postal-card. (The envelope is better, as we frequently wish to reply by a circular or full letter.)*

2. *Do not write for assistance until you have tried to succeed without it.   That is : Do not ask lazy questions. Consult this book and see whether the answer cannot be found within.*

3. *Use the ordinary size and style of writing-paper, and write on only one side of the leaf.*

4. *Give your full address in each letter.   State also the number of the chapter of which you are a member.*

5. *Address all correspondence connected with the organization of new chapters, notices of exchange, and, in fact, concerning the Association in any way, to Mr. H. H. Ballard, 50 South Street, Pittsfield, Mass.*

CHAPTER XVIII.

To conduct the work of a local society of natural history like one of our chapters continuously, with no diminution in the membership, and with no break in the interest, is not the easiest matter in the world ; and those who enter upon the work of the Agassiz Association with the expectation of uninterrupted sunshine are the first to become low-spirited when the inevitable rainy days begin. An intelligent apprehension of the difficulties to be met, and a knowledge of the ways in which these difficulties have been met by others, must be of advantage to all who have recently enrolled themselves among us, and to all who are contemplating that action. A wise man, before beginning to build, sitteth down first and counteth the cost. The first trouble which chapters must expect is loss of members. The chief causes of this loss are three ; and, in the order of their frequency, they are removal from town, loss of interest, death. The population of our country is restless, and ten years is a long time for a family to remain in the same town. This is especially true of the younger members of the family, who go from home to school, from school to college, and from college to business or professional activity. Against loss of members from this cause, and from death, there is no remedy ; and, unless a chapter has taken these inevitable contingencies into previous consideration, it is hard for it to stand the shock of the first removal. The best way to prevent the collapse of a chapter upon the loss of leading members is to have, from the first, a fixed determination to found and establish the chapter as a permanent and self-supporting society ; and not at all as a transient class. Let everything be done with an eye to perpetuity. Let the officers be such persons as are least likely to be called away ; *i. e.*, residents in the town rather than visitors, principals of schools rather than assistants or pupils, persons of steady character and endurance rather than those of vacillating and fitful disposition. Let property be acquired by the chapter as such. A library, a cabinet, a room, a building, all tend to stability. Again, let there be such a system of enlisting desirable members from time to time, especially from the entering classes of schools and colleges, as shall render the chapter continually able to sustain the loss of any who may be obliged to withdraw.

With regard to the third cause of loss, decreasing interest, the remedy is twofold. In the first place, by way of prevention, only such should be received into the society as give reasonable promise of perseverance. It is not usually those who are most easily roused to excited enthusiasm who make the most steadfast workers. Choose rather those who feel their need of knowledge, and are willing to work patiently and persistently to acquire it. Having, then, carefully organized, the utmost care should be taken to have the offices distributed with absolute fairness. Those who are most earnestly zealous for the prosperity of the work, commonly care least about the honors, but should be willing to accept them if offered. The next essential thing is to keep every member at work, not by compulsion, but by providing an abundance of congenial occupation, and by generously recognizing and applauding every faithful effort. It is also indispensable that every member be kept fully informed of the condition and progress of the Agassiz Association at large, and be led to take an active interest in its growth and prosperity. In the second place we must be prepared for inconstancy and defection, to a certain extent, in despite of our most conscientious efforts to maintain interest ; and, when it comes, we must neither be indignant nor discouraged. We must not be indignant, because steady, persevering action is not natural in young persons, but comes as the result of unusual native endowment or of careful training. The interest boys take even in their sports is fitful. They have 'fevers ; '—the baseball fever, the kite fever, the collecting fever, the Agassiz Association fever. Moreover many causes conspire to make the interest less at some times than others,—the fluctuations of the weather, the inequalities of health, the presence of unusual outside attractions, the pressure of approaching examinations. We must not be discouraged, because all these causes of a lack of interest are transient. Baseball will be played just as vigorously when next season comes around ; the now neglected kites are sure to be tugging again at their strings by and by ; the collection, now forgotten and covered with dust, will be cleaned and put in order after a time ; and the interest in our Association work that languishes in December, will certainly bloom again in May. More than this, when the next wave of interest comes, it will come with more staying power ; we shall all be a little older ; we shall have profited by the errors of the past. The best chapters we have to-day, many of them, are chapters that have disbanded once or twice, and once and again reorganized. It is from these considerations that we were led to insert that clause in our rules, by which so long as even *one* member retains his interest, he is allowed to retain the name and number of a chapter, once properly organized, and maintained for six months. Wherever one earnest, faithful, indomitable worker is found, ultimate success is sure. Let us all imitate old Ben Jonson, who said, "When I take the humor of a thing once, I am like your tailor's needle— *I go through.*"

In illustration of the same subject, we print here part of a report recently received from an excellent chapter : "'This programme worked very well for a time, but soon, for some members, the novelty of the thing wore off, and, consequently, their interest began to flag. They still attended the meetings when there were no parties or entertainments to go to, or when their girls could not go walking, but they did not attend the meetings out of any desire to gain knowledge. The few who took an interest in their work did good work ; so good that, in less than six months, we had over three hundred specimens in our cabinet, of which two hundred and eight were labeled and catalogued. We had, besides these, a large number of birds'-eggs and insects. Among other things we counted valuable, were a buffalo's head, and a case of birds worth nearly thirty dollars. We owned a library of excellent books on zoölogy, mineralogy, and entomology. Our meetings we held weekly at my home till October, and after that at a room for which we paid four dollars per month. It certainly seems that, with everything around us helping, and everybody willing to help us, we might have had an excellent chapter. The case was, however, that out of the fifteen active members with which our chapter was blessed, just nine were more of a hindrance than a help. They sometimes condescended to attend the meetings, but when they did so those who wanted to work groaned to themselves and to each other. No one could read an essay or extract, for when he began, all those who did not care for it began to talk and laugh, or box and wrestle. Soon those who wanted to work began to lose heart, and finally, March 25. 1886, just a year, lacking two days, from the day we organized, we disbanded. Still there were four of us who never dropped the idea of having a good chapter in time. Each of our four enthusiasts worked steadily during the summer, one collecting eggs and studying and stuffing birds and collecting insects, another learning to stuff birds, the third collecting minerals, and myself collecting eggs. Two of our members have finished cabinets, made by themselves. Through all our troubles we have had an earnest desire to go on with our studies and form a new chapter, that we might get together once a week and discuss the things of interest we had seen in our rambles. Last Wednesday, January 19, 1887, our new chapter, consisting of four members, held its second meeting at the home of the president, and finished drawing up a constitution. The only officers we now have are a president and secretary. No person can become a member of this chapter without a vote of every member. We are going to make the initiation fee the contribution of one year's subscription to some paper on natural history. We are not going to keep a cabinet, but when any interesting specimen is obtained it is to be brought to the next meeting, and a paper written about the specimen is to be read by the finder. At each meeting the secretary reads from some paper or book an article on natural history, and at the next meeting each member is to read an essay, written from memory, giving as nearly as possible the substance of the article read. In this way we shall remember better the things about which we study. We think that we shall at last succeed. I would like to say to all the chapters that have among their members persons who fool away their time, and who do not respect the desires

and rights of those around them, but spoil their pleasure and steal their profit, that the best thing they can
do for the welfare of their chapter is to put such persons out.   Such persons are worse for a chapter than
all the discouragement and ridicule that can be heaped
upon it by outsiders."

THE SUMMER VACATION.

During July and August most of our schools and
colleges will close their doors, many of those who live
in cities will fasten the shutters, and the Agassiz Association will be let loose along the seashore and in
the forest and fields.   Summer brings her arms full
of leaves and flowers ; the softened earth loosens its
grasp on mineral and fossil ; the air is gay with floating butterflies, and musical with the hum of beetles
and the songs of birds ; nests in shaded thickets hold
dainty secrets ; soft-bodied creatures are slowly mov-
ing their frail and beautiful houses of shell along briny
sands and over spongy moss ; and the warm air and
clear sky continually invite all who are tired of roof
and wall to go out into the larger habitation which is
one continuous doorway all around, and infinite open
window overhead.   With all these advantages of field
study, the vacation is a trying and dangerous season
for many of our chapters.   With the close of school
classes separate, some never to be reunited, few to
come together without some change.   The regular
succession of meetings is interrupted at the best, and
unless the interests of the society are kept in mind
during the summer, there is likely to be more or less
difficulty about reorganizing in the fall.   To avoid
these dangers, let each member keep his thoughts on
the fall reunion while he is away, and try to find as
many interesting specimens as possible to bring back

and exhibit by and by. Some chapters offer little prizes for the best summer work, to be awarded after due examination of specimens and note-books. It is well, too, to remember the General Association, and to strive to make its aims and methods more widely known as we journey from place to place. Some of our young friends establish chapters in almost every place they visit, maintaining also during their absence regular correspondence with their companions who are detained at home. In this way the close of the vacation finds increased, rather than diminished, interest in nature, and the chapter gains a new impulse and enters upon its work with fresh elasticity and vigor.

CHAPTER XIX.

THE badge of the Agassiz Association is the Swiss cross. It is appropriate because Professor Louis Agassiz was born in Switzerland. The number on the badges changes with each chapter, and is the number by which each chapter is known. Mr. Hayward, now of Milford, Mass., has manufactured these badges for us since the beginning of our work, and has given excellent satisfaction. He makes the badges of plain silver and gold, and also, when desired, ornaments them with gems, and makes them into pins and other articles of jewelry. He will furnish an illustrated price-list on application. It is very pleasant to one traveling at a distance to meet a stranger wearing the neat little cross of the A. A., for it frequently leads to a desirable acquaintance.

THE CHARTER.

As each chapter organizes, there is sent to it a certificate of admission, giving its name, number, and letter, together with the date on which its annual report will fall due. Many chapters have expressed a desire for something nicer than this cheap certificate, which is, after all, the best that can be afforded *gratis*, and we have therefore designed and caused to be engraved a charter suitable for framing. It is printed on heavy bond paper, in the manner of a college diploma. At the top is an excellent likeness of Professor Louis Agassiz. This head is from a photograph kindly furnished for this purpose by Mrs. Agassiz, and the reproduction has received her cordial approval. The photograph represents Professor Agassiz seated at a table and looking down, in his intent, penetrating manner, at a sea-urchin which he holds in his hand. The vignette engraving does not of course reproduce the whole figure, but it gives very happily the fine face, and shows us the great naturalist engaged in what was the chief business of his life — personal observation. One great advantage of a handsome charter is that it attracts the immediate attention of all visitors to the rooms of a chapter, and leads to inquiries which often open the way to an invitation to the society. Then, too, it is a constant stimulus to the chapter itself, and a strong bond of union among its members, like a flag to an army of soldiers. This charter is furnished postpaid, for seventy-five cents.

"THE SWISS CROSS."

On the first of January, 1887, the Association obtained what it had long felt the need of, a magazine devoted to its interests. This magazine, which was accepted by unanimous vote as our official organ, was named *The Swiss Cross*, from the badge of the Association. Great credit is due the publisher, Mr. N. D. C. Hodges, who is also the editor of *Science*, for the attractive manner in which *The Swiss Cross* has been printed and illustrated. It has had the effect of uniting our scattered chapters more closely and harmoniously than perhaps any other agency could have done ; it has given ample opportunity for each chapter and member to place on record whatever personal observations or discoveries may have been made, and it has made many persons before unacquainted with the A. A., its friends and helpers. It numbers among its contributors many of America's leading scientists. It should have the cordial support of every member of the society, and of all who wish it well.

Dr. Henry McCook, of Philadelphia, writes of it : " I am very much pleased with *The Swiss Cross.* It promises to be all that we could wish. There is nothing more needed in this generation than a scientific periodical of the kind you propose, which, without being dogmatic, shall be imbued with a reverent and Christian spirit. I shall hope to add to your list by influencing many others to take *The Swiss Cross.* I propose on next Sunday to recommend it from the pulpit to my congregation, which is a very large and influential one."

Members of the A. A. should send immediate notice of any new and interesting observations they may make to the editor, who will also, when desired, receive and forward subscriptions. The price of the magazine is one dollar and a half a year, and it is sent to clubs of six or more for one dollar each.

THE HAND-BOOK.

This little volume has grown in a somewhat peculiar manner. The president of the A. A. kept a record for several years of all the different questions asked him by his correspondents. The answers to these inquiries, arrayed somewhat systematically, constitute this hand-book.

CHAPTER XX.

WHAT, then, is the Agassiz Association as it appears to-day? And what claims has it upon the interest of the public? It is a union of local societies, each numbering from 4 to 120 members, of all ages from 4 to 84. Our total membership is above ten thousand. We are distributed in all the States and Territories with very few exceptions, and have strong branch societies and active members in Canada, England, Ireland, Scotland, France, Chili, and Japan.

The local societies are known as chapters. They take their names from the towns where they are established, and are further distinguished by the letters of the alphabet. Thus the first chapter established in New York City was called New York (A); the second, New York (B), and so on. They also have the privilege, if desired, of adopting such other distinctive names as they may choose, such as 'The Manhattan Chapter,' 'The Hyatt Chapter,' 'The Cuvier Chapter,' etc.

The word 'association' was chosen instead of 'society' from an impression, perhaps not entirely well founded, that that word could be taken to mean 'a union of societies,' just as society means 'a union of individuals.' And our first plan was to have these local societies entirely independent of one another, except in the general name and in the purpose of studying nature. At that time no conventions were thought of, assemblies were not in mind, courses of study had not been contemplated, a badge was not designed, nor had we supposed it possible that thorough scientific work could be systematically done by many of the chapters, if at all.

We chose the name 'Agassiz' because it was then uppermost in mind. His then recent death was fresh in the hearts of the nation ; and his birth in Switzerland, where a similar organization was said to exist, rendered it especially appropriate. The choice was wiser than we knew. No one can read Mrs. Agassiz's life of her husband without feeling that no name could better stimulate us to faithful work.

Having thus selected the name, a letter was sent to Prof. Alexander Agassiz, asking permission publicly to adopt it. Professor Agassiz replied that he "cordially assents that this very pleasant and useful plan for children be called the Agassiz Association, and that we have his hearty good wishes for its success."

The societies that joined us during the first year or two of our existence, when our plans were still uncertain and our methods comparatively crude, retain in many cases the notion that the Agassiz Association to-day is the same loose organization it was at first— an aggregation of local societies united only in name, allowed to drift hither and thither without direction or assistance. But the necessity for careful supervision and guidance has grown more and more apparent. We have been constantly besieged with requests for systematic courses of study, elaborate plans of work, personal counsel and advice. Courses of study have accordingly been added, plans of work sketched, and a regular system of reports established. The conditions of admission have been defined, and, in short, more business-like methods adopted, until we now resemble rather an extended school with numerous classes than an ordinary society.

I may mention four different sorts of chapters.

First, family chapters. The parents and children of a single family unite for joint study and research. Chapters of this sort are especially desirable, and prove almost uniformly permanent. Chapters of another sort are found in schools. There are many teachers able and willing to give their strength and time, beyond the exacting requirements of their contracts, to the encouragement and assistance of their pupils. Under the fostering care of such men and women, the happiest results have been accomplished. Not the least important result is seen in the pleasant personal relations thus established between teacher and pupil. Chapters of a third kind are organized and conducted entirely by young persons. A company of girls or boys meet together and decide to form a branch of the A. A. They elect their officers, draft their rules and by-laws, engage their rooms, build their cabinets, make their collections, prosecute their studies ; and, if I needed to awaken interest or arouse enthusiasm, I should have only to show what our girls and boys have done even when unaided and alone. They have made lists of all the flowers that grow about them, and of all the birds that fly over their heads. They have published papers, started museums, founded libraries. In doing this they have mastered the laws of parliamentary debate ; have learned to observe with accuracy, to write with fluency, to speak with power ; and, after working thus for a few years, many of them have pushed themselves into schools and colleges and laboratories of the highest grade, and are now completing their self-appointed preparation for lives of commanding intelligence and cheerful service. Finally I will mention chapters of adults. In increasing numbers men and women of mature years, feeling the need of that scientific training which the schools of their childhood failed to give, are

organizing societies, joining their influence to our Association, and receiving in return the benefits coming
from united endeavor and from enthusiastic devotion
to a common cause. But, excellent as the work of all
these chapters is, we have found some needed work
beyond their individual attainment. A general con-
vention, for example, could hardly be received and
cared for by a single chapter ; nor could a wide
range of local observations be properly collated and
discussed by the inhabitants of a single town. It has
therefore been deemed wise to bring about the union
of all the chapters of a city or a state into more extended organizations than the single chapter. These con-
federations of chapters are called 'assemblies ; ' the
most prominent at present, January, 1888, being the
State Assemblies of Massachusetts, Iowa and New
Jersey, and the City Assemblies of Philadelphia, Boston, Brooklyn, Chicago, and New York.

Embracing all the chapters, binding into one the
larger and more powerful assemblies, and making
room also for individuals when chapters cannot well
be formed, is our Agassiz Association. And the influence and prosperity of each chapter and assembly can
be increased and perpetuated by spreading everywhere
we go a knowledge of our local work not only, and of
our local organization, but also, and even with more
emphasis, a knowledge of our entire Association, with
its broader membership and its farther-reaching aims.

Our Association is not by any means great or powerful. As yet it is young, it is ignorant, it is weak. We
have no occasion for vain-glory. Yet, on the other
hand, while we have no excuse for vanity, neither need
we feel vexation of spirit. Our purposes are good,
our methods right. In spite of our feebleness, in the
face of our ignorance, critics have been indulgent,
and we have been more encouraged and praised for

what we have tried to do than derided for our failures or censured for our faults. Scientific men of highest repute, men like Ramsay of England, and men like Agassiz, Hyatt, Winchell, Remsen, Gould, Gilman, and Scudder of America, have extended to us the hand of recognition.

The press has almost always been indulgent; and, although we have often exposed ourselves to fair attacks of satire, our real desire to do honest work has turned the most caustic pen to kindness.

In speaking of our helpers, I should be unjust if I failed to mention with renewed gratitude and honor the large number of scientists who have voluntarily devoted their valuable time to the cheerful and patient assistance of our needs. More than fifty gentlemen representing all departments of science hold themselves always ready to answer the questions that puzzle us. Thanks to their benevolence, the boy who lives in the remotest and smallest village can send his bit of stone or his curious beetle to one of these men, and learn its name and history, and, better still, be taught how he may best study by himself its structure and its history. Some of these professors have even volunteered to conduct courses of study in various branches. We have had courses in botany, entomology, and mineralogy.

It seems at first thought difficult, if not impossible, to suggest any general principle of study that can apply to the whole Association, for it is composed of elements so diverse. We are of all ages, of varying capacities and differing desires, living in places widely distant and strangely different. Some of us pick our violets in June, others in January. But there is a common ground on which all stand—love for nature, and desire to learn. And there is one principle that underlies and determines the methods of our study. It is this : Nature must be studied from her own book.

While, therefore, we do not undervalue the printed records of others' work, and while we ever recognize in printed books and papers necessary and cherished guides, yet we believe that our first business is to meet Nature face to face. Therefore we leave the confines of the library and school, and go out under the open sky—into the forest, and along the stream. Forgetting theory and useless wrangling, it is our purpose to see things as they are, and to record them as we see them. It is the business of the Agassiz Association to live for the truth.

Those who first joined our ranks are growing out of childhood into manhood and womanhood. Many adult chapters, too, are forming ; and perhaps to-day one-quarter of our total membership may be over twenty years of age. What can we do for this increasing class ? In the first place we can give them the opportunity to help the younger, even as they themselves have been helped while young. It is to them, the scientists of the future, that we must soon look for special help, instruction, and guidance. Meanwhile we need them still among us to encourage us by their example, and to aid us by their work. And we want to help them, too. We must provide higher courses of study—discover the best books for students more advanced, and help those who need it to secure the best instruction. I was greatly pleased, while resting by the sea, to find in the laboratory at Annisquam, among the twenty-five earnest workers who were bending day after day, and night after night, over the dissecting-table and the microscope, no less than seven men and women who either are or have been members of the Agassiz Association. Here is the moral of it : youthful observation of nature, wisely directed, grows into manly and womanly consecration to science.

Now, one thing our Association ought to do in the near future is to secure control of one or more tables in this and other thoroughly equipped laboratories, and place them year by year freely at the disposal of such of our number as may show themselves worthy. May we not in time hope to establish here and there laboratories of our own, manned by our own professors ?

We wish also to establish courses of study with greater regularity, and of wider range. I should like to see a yearly correspondence course in each of the branches of natural science, conducted by the best teachers of America. I should wish these courses, specimens included, to be absolutely free ; and I should wish the men who give them well paid for their time and work.

At present, as we depend entirely upon volunteers, our courses, though frequent, are rather desultory, and accompanied with some slight expense for specimens and printing. To do all we hope to do will cost much money, and the money must be raised. The Agassiz Association must be endowed, and the money will come, as time and devoted labor have long since come. There are plenty of wealthy men and women ready to give money as soon as we can prove that it can be given safely, worthily and well. Now, here we have a school of more than ten thousand pupils, confined to no one city, no one State, no one denomination. We have a corps of fifty volunteer instructors. We need no expensive buildings. And if we find that in order to meet the needs of our maturing membership we need a fund of ten or twenty or fifty thousand dollars, whose income shall be applied to giving worthy young men and women a chance to work under competent instruction, I have faith to believe that some man will be found deep enough in pocket, and broad enough in heart, to endow the Agassiz Association as he might a collegiate chair or a private school. Let each chapter and each member be like Diogenes, ever peering about with lighted lantern to find this man.

But we need not wait for that. There is enough we can do unaided ; and, indeed, I am inclined to think that labor voluntarily expended by boys and girls in building their own cabinets, and by girls in decorating and caring for their assembly-rooms, is the cause of the truest satisfaction and enjoyment, and is also productive of the greatest interest in the weightier matters of scientific study. You can see most clearly through a microscope that you have worked and waited for.

If the endowment ought to come, it will come in due time ; but in the meanwhile let each continue to do his best where he happens to be. The way to help the whole Association is to give your best attention to your individual work. Let the little ones gather their pebbles and their flowers. Let the elder look more closely into the structure and the habits of bird, or beast, or plant. Let us all be always living for the truth, and striving to read in every leaf of Nature's book her lesson of faith, her lesson of hope, her lesson of love.

Admirably has one of our Iowa chapters united science and humanity. Organized as a society of scientific workers, it has made itself also a band of mercy. It has proved that, although the eye of Science is keen, her heart need not be cold, and that her hand, however cunning, may yet be kind. Two kindred spirits were Agassiz and Audubon ; and very many who, with us, have enrolled themselves under the name 'Agassiz,' have also joined the Audubon Society, while many others are learning — regarding birds not only, but every living thing—never needlessly to hurt or to destroy.

What, after all, is our purpose in studying Nature? Is it to get for ourselves collections of rare and beautiful objects? Is it to amuse us during our leisure hours? Is it to train our powers of observation and strengthen our minds by careful discipline? Is it to satisfy our natural thirst for knowledge, and to become familiar with all the little strangers of the roadside and the wood? It is all this, but it should be much more. We ought to be learning the grand and solemn lesson that a Divine mind is showing its wisdom in every leaf and pebble, and that a Divine heart is expressing its love in every raindrop and in every flower. This was the truth that filled the heart of him for whom our Association is named—this was the secret of his untiring zeal, and the key to his deep love of Nature. It has grown to be a pleasant custom for our chapters to celebrate Professor Agassiz's birthday (May 28), by means of an excursion or picnic, combined with appropriate literary exercises ; and perhaps on such an occasion nothing will more truly bring home to us the sweet spirit of the great naturalist than Whittier's poem, 'The Prayer of Agassiz ; ' or Longfellow's lines on his fiftieth birthday, which, by the courtesy of his publishers, we are able to reproduce.

THE FIFTIETH BIRTHDAY OF AGASSIZ.

MAY 28, 1867.

It was fifty years ago,
  In the pleasant month of May,
In the beautiful Pays de Vaud,
  A child in its cradle lay.

And Nature, the old nurse, took
  The child upon her knee,
Saying :   "Here is a story-book
  Thy Father has written for thee."

"Come, wander with me," she said,
  "Into regions yet untrod,
And read what is still unread
  In the manuscripts of God."

And he wandered away and away
  With Nature, the dear old nurse,
Who sang to him night and day
  The rhymes of the universe.

And whenever the way seemed long,
  Or his heart began to fail,
She would sing a more wonderful song,
  Or tell a more marvelous tale.

So she keeps him still a child,
  And will not let him go,
Though at times his heart beats wild
  For the beautiful Pays de Vaud ;

Though at times he hears in his dreams
  The Ranz des Vaches of old,
And the rush of mountain streams
  From glaciers clear and cold ;

And the mother at home says, "Hark !
  For his voice I listen and yearn ;
It is growing late and dark,
  And my boy does not return."

CHAPTER XXI.

HINTS AND HELPS FOR AGASSIZ ASSOCIATION WORKERS.

SPECIAL attention is invited to the following works, selected at random from the catalogue of Messrs. Cassell & Company, Limited, of New York, London, Paris and Melbourne. A complete descriptive catalogue of their publications will be forwarded free to any address on application. Their new address is 104 and 106 Fourth Avenue, New York.

"European Ferns : their Form, Habit, and Culture," by James Britten, F.L.S., Department of Botany, British Museum, with 30 fac-simile colored illustrations from Nature, by D. Blair, F.L.S., and over 120 wood blocks, aims at giving a plain and intelligible account of European Ferns. Price, $7.50.

"The Fresh Water Fishes of Europe : a History of their Genera, Species, Structure, Habit, and Distribution," by H. G. Seeley, F.R.S., F.G.S., F.Z.S., F.L.S., F.R.G.S., is an elegant volume of nearly 450 pages, containing 214 illustrations. In this volume the fresh water fishes of Europe are systematically described for the first time. Price, $5.00.

"European Butterflies and Moths," with 61 colored plates based upon Bergis' "Schmetterlingsbuch." By W. F. Kirby, Assistant in the Zoölogical Department, British Museum, and Secretary of the Entomological Society of London. This volume contains a full and complete index to English names and index of genera and species, and is issued in one large quarto volume. Price, $15.00.

The works of Louis Figuiers, issued by this house at reduced price, demand special attention. The seven volumes in this set contain over 2,250 illustrations, and are published at $1.50 per volume, or $10.50 for the set. The volumes may be had separate, viz. : "The Human Race," with 242 illustrations ; "The Insect World," 570 illustrations ; "Mammalia," 260 illustrations ; "The Ocean World," 427 illustrations ; "Reptiles and Birds," 307 illustrations ; "The Vegetable World," 470 illustrations ; "The World before the Deluge," 233 illustrations.

Among the many exquisite portfolios which we notice on their catalogue are "Wild Flowers of the Rocky Mountains," a selection of 24 of the finest wild flowers, from original water-colors, done in from 12 to 15 colors. These are put up in three boxes, eight plates to each box. Per box, $1.50.

"Wild Birds Portfolio." A selection of 40 beautifully colored plates put up in two handsome boxes, 20 plates in each box. Price per box, $1.50.

Their list includes "Garden Flower Portfolios," 4 boxes, 20 plates in each box, at $1.50 each; "Wild Flower Portfolios," 6 boxes, 20 plates in each box, at $1.50 each; "Flower Garden Portfolio," 3 boxes, 12 plates 9 x 12 in each box, at $1.50 each.

In selecting books for reference and study, members of the Agassiz Association cannot do better than consult the classified and descriptive catalogue of D. Appleton & Co. (New York).

Besides the works of such masters in scientific investigation as Darwin, Figuier, Huxley, Herbert Spencer, Tyndall, Proctor, and others, they publish a number of important books in almost every branch of scientific study. Their "Scientific Primers" are noteworthy attempts to convey information in such a manner as to make it both intelligible and interesting to beginners.

A series of elementary works on mechanical and physical science are published under the general heading of "Text-books of Science." These books are practical treatises, sound and exact in their logic, and illustrated by well-selected examples from familiar processes and facts.

Mention should also be made of their well-known "International Scientific Series," which consists of sixty or more large volumes, covering a wide range of scientific research, and forming quite a respectable library in itself.

In glancing through the catalogue, we find many titles which are sure to excite an interest in the minds of the younger members of the Association.

The "Fairy Land of Science," for instance, or "Life and Her Children," and "Winners in Life's Race," by Arabella B. Buckley, are sure of an interested audience in whosoever's hands they may fall. Then we have "A World of Wonders; or, Marvels in Animate and Inanimate Nature," wherein many curious tales are told of marine and vegetable life and the insect and reptile world; "Light Science for Leisure Hours," a series of familiar essays on scientific subjects, natural phenomena, etc.; Dr. Abbott's "A Naturalist's Rambles About Home," which tells of country walks and studies of the habits of the wild creatures of our woods and fields; Sir John Lubbock's "Ants, Bees and Wasps," containing the record of various experiments made with ants, bees and wasps during a period of ten years, with a view of testing their mental condition and powers of sense; P. H. Gosse's "Evenings at the Microscope;" Grant Allen's "Flowers and their Pedigrees;" and many others equally interesting.

The most recent of their publications is Sir William Dawson's "Geological History of Plants," which aims to give in a connected form a summary of the development of the vegetable kingdom in geological time.

The great "American Cyclopædia," the "Cyclopædia of American Biography," and the "Popular Science Monthly," are also published by Messrs. Appleton & Co.

Besides their large list of works for the general reader on scientific subjects, Messrs. Appleton & Co. publish a number of excellent text-books for special study. These books will most interest the working members in the Association and help them to a practical knowledge of the subjects in which they are engaged.

Those interested in the study of chemistry will find Mary Shaw-Brewster's "First Book of Chemistry" a great help in making experiments. As all the experiments are elementary in character, only the simplest apparatus and chemicals are needed. Another useful book just published is J. D. Everett's "Outlines of Natural Philosophy," in which the leading principles of that branch of science are presented in the plainest manner.

Eliza A. Bowen's "Astronomy by Observation" is based, as its title implies, on the interesting, as it is, indeed, the only true method of studying the subject—that of observation. Careful directions are given when, how and where to find the heavenly bodies, together with many curious facts concerning them.

Eliza A. Youmans' "First Book of Botany" is an excellent text-book for a beginner in that interesting study, taking the learner by the hand and leading him among the plants themselves to find out their history. "A Study of Leaves," by Mary B. Dennis, is also a useful companion.

For students in Zoölogy we commend Dr. Edward S. Morse's "First Book of Zoölogy." The examples presented in this book are the common and familiar animals. The illustrations, of which there are upwards of three hundred, were nearly all drawn from nature by the author expressly for this work.

The "Science Text-book Series," contains a number of important books for more advanced work, in Descriptive and Physiological Botany, Geology, Zoölogy, Chemistry," etc., etc.

The Agassiz Association owes Messrs. Appleton & Co. a vote of thanks for the delightful way in which young people are introduced to their animal friends in James Johonnot's series of Natural History Readers. The "Book of Cats and Dogs," and "Friends in Feathers and Fur," are sure to bring recruits to the Association from the ranks of the little folks, while older heads will find something of the charm of looking through the author's spectacles in " Neighbors with Wings and Fins," " Some Curious Flyers, Creepers and Swimmers," " Neighbors with Claws and Hoofs," " The Animate World," etc.

D. Appleton & Co., No. 3 Bond Street, New York, will send their complete catalogue of publications to any member of the Association on request.

" Insect Lives ; or, Born in Prison," is the title of a most delightful book for young people, by Mrs. Julia P. Ballard, a copy of which should be in the hands of every member of the Agassiz Association. Every boy and girl who gets hold of it will at once begin a careful investigation of the habits and manners of all the caterpillars and butterflies which come within reach. Mrs. Ballard has a rare faculty of interesting her readers and imparting a vast deal of information, while she is disclosing the secrets of the prison-houses of these wonderful little creatures. If you are at all interested in the curious history of moths, caterpillars, butter-flies, and other members of their family ; if you want to know where they come from, how they live, what they do and where they go, then you want to get this book without delay. The book is handsomely and beautifully illustrated, and may be had of all booksellers, or will be sent, post-free, by The Writers Publishing Company, 21 University Place, New York, on receipt of $1.00.

No American scientist has ever left on record so large a list of standard works in his chosen department as did the late Professor Asa Gray on the subject of botany. His " How Plants Grow " remains at the present time as it was when first issued, the *par excellence* of elementary text-books. It is probably more largely used now than ever before, and this despite the fact that it has had almost numberless competitors which have arisen from time to time, and have fallen into merited disuse, while the " How Plants Grow " still remains apparently as fresh and popular as ever.

" Gray's Lessons in Botany, Revised," the last work issued before the author's death, is of a higher grade than the "How Plants Grow," but perhaps equally desirable in its way. This book, with the added " Field, Forest and Garden Botany," constitutes the well-known " School and Field Book," which is the book specially adapted for high schools, academies, and seminaries of the first class, and for individual learners not pursuing the study of botany as a specialty. For such students, there are the " Gray's Structural Botany" and " Goodale's Physiological Botany"—these two being parts of " Gray's New Botanical Text-book," in four volumes, the concluding volumes having been left incomplete by the death of the author. These, however, it is understood, will be finished by his disciples and friends, who were in full sympathy with Dr. Gray and his work, and conversant with his plans.

Professor Coulter, of Wabash College, a man who stood high in Dr. Gray's regard, has prepared a "Manual of the Botany of the Rocky Mountains," which, being the only published flora of its locality, is well-nigh indispensable to Western students. This work, prefaced by "Gray's Revised Lessons," mentioned above, comprises a complete introduction, grammar, and lexicon of the subject for use in the West. For the special student and the library, "Gray's Synoptical Flora" is well-nigh indispensable. This was looked upon by the author as his life-work. The Gamopetalous Dicotyledons are issued complete in one volume. Other sections of the work are understood to be ready for the printer, but the concluding parts will be left to other hands to finish.

Gray's Botanists' Microscopes, with either two or three lenses, are admirably adapted to their purpose, and can be safely recommended to learners.

It is attached to a box, one and a half inches high, and less than four inches long, into which it is neatly folded when not in use. The needles are used for dissecting flowers or other objects too small to be otherwise handled for analysis. The lenses magnify about *fifteen* diameters ; or, with three lenses, about one-third more.

Dr. Gray's entire series of botanical text-books, a part of which is described above, is published by Messrs. Ivison, Blakeman & Co., New York and Chicago.

No reference book should be more freely consulted than Webster's Unabridged Dictionary. Its definitions of scientific words are unequaled, and in all other departments of lexicographic research it stands pre-eminent. It defines three thousand more words than any other dictionary published in this country. Thirty-six State superintendents of schools and over one hundred college presidents recommend it. It is the standard authority in the U. S. Supreme Court and in the Government printing-office.

Little Flower People, by Gertrude E. Hale, presents fundamental botanical facts in a fanciful dress, arousing interest and stimulating observation. Illustrated. 50 cents. A Primer of Botany, by A. A. Knight, brings the subject to the level of intermediate grades, and is especially valuable as an introduction to physiological botany. Illustrated. 35 cents. Published by Ginn & Co., Boston.

The authority of Dr. Henry C. McCook, of Philadelphia, as an investigator in entomology has been strengthened and extended by his charming volume, "Tenants of an Old Farm : Leaves from the Note-Book of a Naturalist." It describes a series of excursions afield, with inquiries into the appearance, dispositions and habits of bees, ants, spiders, crickets, moths, and a great variety of insects, detailed in a scientifically accurate but familiar and fascinating style. Numerous well-engraved original illustrations, after drawings from nature (except some comical character-drawings by Dan Beard, showing the humorous side of insect life), add much to the instructive value of the work. 460 pp., well indexed, $2.50. Will be mailed to any member of the Agassiz Association on receipt of $2.00 by the publishers, Fords, Howard & Hulbert, 27 Park Place, New York.

Every Chapter of the association, in its library, small or large, should secure the best works for reference on subjects in which it is interested. BRADLEE WHIDDEN, 41 Arch street, Boston, publishes some valuable books on birds and taxidermy, insects, mammals, the microscope, botany, mosses, lichens, algæ, shells, marine life, minerals, and kindred subjects, which workers sometimes need. Maynard's "Butterflies of New England," with 232 colored plates, $7.00; Brooks' "Hand-book of Invertebrate Zoölogy," $3.00; Behrens' "Guide to the Microscope in Botany," $5.00; Whitman's "Methods in Anatomy and Embryology," $3.00, bear heavy-sounding names, but are most useful and instructive. Haeckel's "Visit to Ceylon," $1.75; "Manual of Taxidermy," $1.25; "Birds' Nesting," $1.25; "Naturalist's Assistant," $1.50; "Life on the Seashore," $1.50, are just as useful and easy to understand. Catalogues sent to any one on application, or these books can be had through all booksellers.

Mr. George O. Simmons, No. 352 Gates avenue, Brooklyn, N. Y., has prepared two very complete collections of minerals, which are arranged in cases in convenient form for reference. One of these, prepared expressly for the entertainment and instruction of children in schools and families, is the "Diamond" Mineral Collection, 10 x 6 inches in size. This collection consists of fifty natural mineral specimens (mostly of the industrial varieties), classified according to the system recommended by Prof. J. D. Dana, in his "Manual of Mineralogy." It contains fifty specimens, arranged in a neat pasteboard box, the names of the species being printed underneath. The specimens are all of good quality and size, and exhibit well the characteristics of the minerals. A neat eight-page descriptive manual goes with the collection, the price of which is $1.50, postpaid. The same collection, consisting entirely of massive (uncrystallized) specimens, furnished for $1.00. The "Student's Complete Mineral Collection" is one of great extent and variety, and is accompanied by

Dana's Revised " Manual of Mineralogy and Petrography " for reference purposes. It comprises 300 species and sub-species, includes most of the salient and many of the rare minerals described in Dana's manual. It contains cubes, octahedrons, dodecahedrons, trapezohedrons, cleavages of rhombic and hexagonal prisms, and crystallizations of the minerals which occur only, or mainly, in crystallized form. Many of the specimens illustrate to perfection the property of cleavage. In massive specimens, numbers of the objects are duplicated, to show not only the contrasts in colors which the same mineral often possesses, but also other differences between individuals of the same species taken from different localities. The specimens are arranged in the center of a square space, with the name of the species printed at the bottom. The numbers on the left are consecutive, and those on the right indicate the pages of the manual on which the descriptions are given. The specimens are of good size, and are quite characteristic of the species. The prices of this collection are as follows : No. 1, polished black walnut case ; edges and corners rounded ; six drawers, which are secured by a hinged side, in which is fitted a lock and key ; size 12 x 6½ x 7½, $30.00. No. 2, six pasteboard trays, with wooden sides ; contained in a strong box, also of pasteboard ; size 12 x 6½ x 4¾, $25. The collections are furnished without the manual for $2.00 less. Should the collection not be accepted by the purchaser, it may be returned, in which event the remittance will be refunded, less cost of transportation. Mr. Simmons will also furnish single specimens of any size consistent with the nature and rarity of the minerals wanted. His collections are indorsed by some of the highest authorities in mineralogical science. Circulars giving detailed information will be mailed by him on application.

A perfect understanding of zoölogy and mineralogy is best obtained by the examination of representative specimens, correctly named and located. James M. Southwick, Providence, R. I., U. S. A., is very particular in the preparation and furnishing of mineralogical specimens, shells and eggs, also birds and mammals, both mounted and in skins. He has also for sale all the tools required by zoölogical and botanical students. Circulars sent on application.

The study of microscopy is one in which an increasing number of persons are yearly becoming interested. Societies for the study of this delightful branch of science are springing up in all parts of the country, and, like the Agassiz Association, their necessity demands an organ which will give not only information and instruction in this subject, but will also furnish society reports and general information in microscopy. Such a journal is The Microscope, a thirty-two-page illustrated monthly, filled with just the matter of most interest to the amateur or professional microscopist. Subscription, $1.00 a year, with 1,700 microscopical slides as premium to select from. Sample free. The Microscope Publishing Co., 25 Washington avenue, Detroit, Mich.

By its enlargement of our natural powers of sight (almost, indeed, conferring a new sense), the microscope is an invaluable aid in the study of nature near at hand. As reliable manufacturers, we can recommend the firm of Jas. W. Queen & Co., 924 Chestnut street, Philadelphia, who publish a catalogue of microscopes which those interested would do well to send for ; they are always glad to advise with intending purchasers regarding the choice of a suitable instrument. A pocket magnifier, at least, is indispensable to the student ; these are illustrated and described in the catalogue above referred to. Botanical collecting cases, with sling strap, are supplied (in two sizes) by this firm ; also plant presses. Insect pins, in all sizes, and sheet cork may also be obtained at Queen's.

The American Naturalist, an illustrated monthly, devoted to natural sciences in their widest sense, is published at $4.00 per annum, 40 cents per number, by Leonard Scott Publishing Co., Philadelphia, Pa.

Every member of the Agassiz Association can have the POPULAR SCIENCE NEWS sent to them one year for fifty cents only. The regular price is $1.00. The best and cheapest journal of popular science published in the world. It includes among its regular contributors Professors Young of Princeton, Shaler of Harvard, Sumner of Yale, Dr. D. G. Brinton of Philadelphia, Dr. Varigny of Paris, France, and many other prominent scientists. Send a fifty-cent postal note to the publishers, or else your address on a postal card for a free sample copy and full particulars. Address Popular Science News Co., 19 Pearl street, Boston, Mass.

Those interested in the study of bees, wasps, ichneumon-flies, etc., should obtain a copy of the Synopsis of the families and genera of the Hymenoptera of America north of Mexico, by E. T. Cresson, containing synoptic tables of the genera, also a catalogue of all the species that have been described, and a list of the works and papers that have been published on the subject. 350 pp., 8vo, 1887. Published by the American Entomological Society, at Philadelphia, Pa., by whom a list of other entomological publications for sale will be sent on application.

The Auk, a Quarterly Journal of Ornithology, is an indispensible magazine for all interested in ornithology It consists entirely of original matter, much of it more or less popular in character. While primarily devoted to North American ornithology, its department of reviews gives notices of all important general works on birds, as well as a full record of all publications relating to the ornithology of North America. Published at $3.00 per year for the American Ornithologists' Union, by L. S. Foster, 35 Pine street, New York City.

The classification of every North American bird, with its popular and scientific names, and a brief statement of where it is found, is given in "The American Ornithologists' Union Check-List of North American Birds." This list was prepared by a committee of five of our most distinguished ornithologists, and is the recognized standard authority on the subject. Price $3.00. Address L. S. Foster, 35 Pine street, New York City.

"The Manual of the Vertebrates of the Northern United States," by Dr. David S. Jordan, includes a great body of compact descriptions of vertebrates, and classifies them by a system more known to botanists than zoölogists. It is indispensable to the amateur zoölogist. $2.50. A. C. McClurg & Co., Chicago, publishers.

"Science Sketches," by Dr. David S. Jordan, President Indiana University, is one of the best books on popular science lately published. It includes "The Story of a Salmon," "Johnny Darters," "The Salmon Family," "Dispersion of Fresh Water Fishes," "The Story of a Stone," "Darwin," "The Ascent of the Matterhorn," etc., etc. The style is charming, and the book is delightful as well as profitable. $1.50. Published by A. C. McClurg & Co.

For a general family cyclopedia we recommend, from personal experience, the International Cyclopedia, published by Dodd & Mead, New York.

If one loves botany he should subscribe for some journal that will keep him informed of the progress of the science, of the new discoveries being made, that will describe the places and the persons that have become famous in connection with the science, and that will give methods of preserving and studying plants; such a journal, for instance, as the Botanical Gazette, published at Crawsfordsville, Ind., which is an illustrated monthly costing two dollars a year. It is particularly newsy and readable, yet holds a high place among botanical journals.

Frank H. Laitin, of Albion, Orleans Co., N. Y., is a dealer in natural history specimens, instruments, supplies, and publications of all kinds. Every A. A. Chapter should have a copy of his complete catalogue and price-lists before making purchases. His specimens are the very best, and his prices will be found to be much lower than those of any other reliable dealer.

The Naturalists' Bureau, Salem, Mass., are prepared to furnish mounting paper (fine quality, heavy weight and standard size) for $4.75 per ream ; genus covers, $2.75 per hundred ; driers at $1.00 per hundred, or $4.50 per bundle of five hundred, and also scientific books and instruments. Send for catalogue and samples.

"The Booklover's Rosary," being the Praise of Books in the words of about one hundred of the most famous writers, of all ages, from Socrates to Saxe, followed by "The Literary Revolution" catalogue of choice books in every department of literature —books published at the lowest prices ever known—the whole forming a quarto volume of 132 pages, will be sent free to any member of the Agassiz Association who will send request therefor to John B. Alden, Publisher, 393 Pearl street, New York, or 218 Clarke street, Chicago, Ill.

Many members of the Association use with profit Shaler's First Book in Geology ($1.00) ; Crosby's Common Minerals and Rocks (40 cts.) ; Colton's Practical Zoölogy (80 cts.) ; Hyatt's About Pebbles (10 cts.) ; Commercial and Other Sponges (20 cts.) ; Corals and Echinoderms (20 cts.) ; Mollusca (25 cts.) ; Worms and Crustacea (25 cts.) ; Goodale's Few Common Plants (15 cts.) ; Richard's First Lessons in Minerals (10 cts.) ; Agassiz's First Lesson in Natural History (20 cts.) ; and Clarke's How to Find the Stars (15 cts.). These books are published by D. C. Heath & Co., Boston.

"First Steps in Scientific Knowledge," of which Paul Bert, ex-Minister of Education in France, is the author, is published by the J. B. Lippincott Company, of Philadelphia. The translation of the work into English was done by Madame Paul Bert, and in the American edition such changes and additions have been made as were needed to adapt the work to American schools. The additions include all common and important American species of animals and plants. Each lesson is given in a conversational form, rendering it both interesting and familiar, and sustaining the attention of the pupil. The numerous illustrations (550) are accompanied by explanatory notes. The experiments in physics and chemistry require only such apparatus as can be found in any community or purchased at the nearest store. The price of the complete volume is 60 cents.

The Baker & Taylor Co., 740 and 742 Broadway, New York, can supply ANY *of the works contained in*

*the list of " Books Recommended," and offer liberal dis-
counts on large orders. They deal in both miscellaneous
and school books, and carry one of the largest and most
varied collections of books in the country. They are
always ready to furnish inquirers, either personally or
by mail, with information about current miscellaneous
and educational publications.*